ISO 9000

ISO 9000

A Comprehensive Guide to Registration,

Audit Guidelines, and Successful Certification

Greg Hutchins

THE OLIVER WIGHT COMPANIES

Oliver Wight

Oliver Wight Publications, Inc.
5 Oliver Wight Drive
Essex Junction, Vermont 05452-9985

CONTENTS

ACKNOWLEDGMENTS

THANK YOU: To the many people who helped me with this book. Your contributions made this a much better product. Finally, for any nonconformances (to use a quality term), I take sole responsibility.

- Maureen Breitenberg, NIST

- Lee Buddress, Portland State University professor

- Bruce Campbell, ISO Specialties

- Jim Childs, Oliver Wight Publications

- Amiram Daniel, Olympus Corp.

- Harry Gundlach, Raad voor de Certificate (RvC)

- Jim Highlands, Management Systems Analysis

- Charles Hyer, The Marley Organization

- Patricia Kopp, ASQC

- Gary Lewis, Amoco Performance Products

- Horacio Martirena, Argentine consultant

- Henri Mitonneau, Amovi

- John Nolan, UNC

- Charles Packard, Paramax
- Daryl Parker, A.G.A. Quality
- Nils Ringstedt, The National Swedish Board for Consumer Policies
- Chuck Russo, A.G.A. Quality
- Les Schnoll, Dow Corning
- Miles Seaman, Lloyd's Register
- Norm Siefert, White-Rodgers
- C. A. J. Simons, Philips

PREFACE

Proofread EVERYTHING, dummy!
—THOMAS BRAZELL,
U.S. Army Material Command

Why is ISO 9000 so hot? The ISO 9000 logic goes as follows:

- Jobs, jobs, jobs are the major public-policy issue in the 1990s.

- Economic competitiveness has displaced military competitiveness.

- Competitiveness $\Longleftrightarrow$ Quality

- U.S. growth is flat. Overseas economic growth is strong.

- ISO 9000 is an internationally accepted standard for accessing markets, ensuring quality products, and building trust among trade partners.

Whether one agrees with the above logic, the fact is that ISO 9000 quality series of standards through acceptance and usage is becoming an important part of the global business landscape.

You may be considering ISO registration to improve your organization's efficiency, effectiveness, or economics. Or, your customer or your competition is already pursuing ISO registration. This book demonstrates how you can take advantage of becoming registered.

In addition to presenting the political and economic background, this book will help you understand the language, processes, systems, technology, and requirements of ISO 9000. And if you intend to pursue registration, this book provides information on how to get started and outlines the steps and the best way to do it at a low cost. Finally, the basic premise of this book is that registration should only be pursued if it adds value to your company.

You are my customer. If you have success stories, tips, or ideas on ISO 9000, I'd like to hear from you.

GREG HUTCHINS
Quality Plus Engineering
Portland, Oregon
(800) COMPETE

ISO 9000

CHAPTER 1

Introducing ISO 9000:
Questions and Answers

The secret of business is to know something that nobody else knows.
—ARISTOTLE ONASSIS

WHAT IS ISO?

ISO is the International Organization for Standardization, and its objective is to promote the development of standards, testing, and certification in order to encourage the trade of goods and services. The organization consists of representatives from ninety-one countries. Each country is represented by a standards body. The American National Standards Institute (ANSI), for example, is the U.S. representative to ISO. ANSI is a standards organization that facilitates the development of consensus standards in the U.S. It does not develop or write standards. It provides a structure and mechanism for industry or product groups to come together to establish consensus and develop a standard.

ISO comprises more than 180 technical committees, covering many industry sectors and products. The American Society for Quality Control (ASQC) administers the U.S. Technical Advisory Group (TAG), which presents its views to the

3

international ISO technical committee. The U.S. TAG to ISO Technical Committee 176 consists of quality experts that work with the international committee to draft, revise, and word ISO 9000 quality assurance and quality management documents.

WHAT IS QUALITY?

ISO Standard 8402 explains critical terms relating to quality. *Quality* is defined as: "The totality of features and characteristics of a product or service that bear on its ability to satisfy stated or implied needs." This approach, while acceptable, does not incorporate many of the latest interpretations of quality.

The concept of quality has changed dramatically over the last ten years and even more so during the last two years. A decade ago, the emphasis focused on products; that is, quality meant a product's ability to conform to specifications. Later its definition started to incorporate elements of the customer, and quality was defined as "anticipating and exceeding customer expectations."

In the last several years, *the concept of quality has evolved to recognize the importance of satisfying an organization's many stakeholders, including community, suppliers, shareholders, employees, and management.* Quality now includes such diverse elements as improving work life, promoting workplace diversity, bettering environmental conditions, facilitating trade, and enhancing competitiveness.

WHAT IS MEANT BY QUALITY SYSTEM AND TOTAL QUALITY MANAGEMENT?

Two additional fundamental concepts used throughout this book are *quality system* and *Total Quality Management*. ISO Standard 8402 defines quality system as: "The organizational structure, responsibilities, procedures, processes, and resources needed to implement quality management." ISO 9000 specifies requirements for quality systems. Total Quality Management (TQM) is defined as: "A management approach to an organization centered on quality, based on the participation of all its members and aiming at long-term success through customer satisfaction, and benefits to the members of the organization and to society."[1]

[1] Definitions are from ISO Standard 8402, "Quality Management and Quality Assurance—Vocabulary," 1991, p. 17.

Several important points can be derived from these concepts. Long-term success through customer satisfaction is an organization's goal and is predicated on the pursuit of quality, everyone's participation, and value to society.

Your customer's requirements must first be identified, defined, and clarified. Procedures and systems are then established to monitor, control, and improve those variables that directly and indirectly are involved in the production of uniform products and the delivery of consistent services.

WHAT ARE ISO 9000 SERIES STANDARDS?

ISO 9000 is a series of five international standards on quality management and assurance. The series consists of ISO 9000, ISO 9001, ISO 9002, ISO 9003, and ISO 9004. ISO 9000 is a road map for implementing ISO 9001, ISO 9002, or ISO 9003. These three quality standards can be thought of in terms of their differences in scope. The most comprehensive, ISO 9001, incorporates all twenty quality elements of the quality standard; ISO 9002 has eighteen of the elements; and ISO 9003 has the twelve basic elements. (These are shown in the sidebar on page 77.)

ISO 9001 is used by companies to certify their quality systems throughout the product-development cycle, from design to service. It includes the product-design element, which is becoming more critical to customers that rely on error-free products.

ISO 9002 is used by companies for whom the focus is on production and installation. This quality standard may be used by a company whose products have already been marketed, tested, improved, and approved. Chances are the product quality is high. These companies focus their quality efforts on maintaining and improving existing quality systems, instead of developing quality systems for a new product.

ISO 9003 is for companies in which comprehensive quality systems may not be important or necessary, such as commodity suppliers. In these cases, final product inspection and testing would suffice.

The above functional criteria for selecting the appropriate ISO standard are broad. The following are additional criteria to consider when selecting the appropriate standard with which to comply:

- Design-process capability

- Design maturity

- Production-process capability

- Product or service characteristics

- Product or service safety

- Economics[2]

ISO 9000 to ISO 9004 quality standards in the U.S. are called ANSI/ASQC Q90 to Q94. Most countries refer to the standards differently (see sidebar on page 72); however, they are technically equivalent. You can get a working knowledge of the quality standards by referring to the appendix, which shows a typical quality manual of a fictional organization pursuing ISO 9001. Quality auditors will work off this typical manual when conducting the audit.

ISO 9001/9002/9003 are contractual documents in which a customer requires certification or compliance by a supplier. The language in these standards prescribes compliance in "shall" language. ISO 9004 and a number of other similar ISO documents describe recommended quality actions or guidelines in "should" language. This book focuses on the ISO 9001/9002/9003, the "shall" compliance (or commonly called conformance) standards.

ISO 9000 series quality standards can be purchased through the American Society for Quality Control (ASQC) or the American National Standards Institute (ANSI). (Addresses and phone numbers can be found in the Resources section on page 237.)

ARE THE STANDARDS EASY TO UNDERSTAND AND TO IMPLEMENT?

The standards are easy to use if a company already has a quality program. ISO quality terms and concepts are elementary and widely accepted in the quality universe. The standards are also abbreviated; for example, ISO 9001 quality standard is only seven pages. However, it is basically a "one size fits all" type of issue. The standards were developed to be generic and applicable to companies in most industry sectors. As a result, the standards are often not easy to implement or to shoehorn into a specific process, system, or industry. But with effort and ingenuity, ISO 9000 quality standards can be applied broadly and fine-tuned to the specific application, process, or product.

The basic purpose of the quality series standards is for a company to be able to establish quality systems, maintain product integrity, and satisfy the customer.

---

[2] "ISO 9000: Quality Management and Quality Assurance Standards—Guidelines for Use," Geneva, Switzerland. 1987. p. 4.

And, in the process of using the standards, a company will develop internal self-discipline and a greater understanding of the purposes and benefits of quality management.

Many deficiencies with the current series of standards are being remedied through ISO implementation guidance documents, some of which are presently available. (Others are being drafted.) These guidance documents cover quality systems, techniques, and products. For example, specific guidance documents are being developed for processed materials, software, quality improvement, and project management.

WHAT ARE THE MAJOR CHALLENGES WITH ISO 9000?

ISO 9001/9002/9003 have some deficiencies that are being addressed and will be corrected in future revisions. However, a mention of these shortcomings can illuminate the broader scope of subsequent ISO 9000 revisions. Issues to be dealt with specifically are: continuous improvement, external or internal customer satisfaction, quality metrics, culture and other organizational factors.

WHAT IS DRIVING INTERNATIONAL ISO 9000 ADOPTION?

ISO 9000 is like a virus. Its adoption and acceptance is seemingly growing in an uncontrolled fashion. Why?

Several reasons are:

- dissolution of the former Soviet Union

- global emphasis on economic competitiveness

- economic power of the European Community (EC)

- worldwide emphasis on quality

- universal acceptance of ISO 9000

- U.S. intent to supplant military quality standards with ISO 9000

DOES ISO REGISTRATION GET YOUR PRODUCT INTO THE EUROPEAN COMMUNITY?

Not necessarily! For U.S. exporters the key is to understand the new European Community (EC) directives, which state specific product safety requirements. ISO 9000 registration is not a legal requirement or a preferred option for entry to the EC market. ISO registration may not simply be a stand-alone quality requirement. The manufacturer of regulated products has different options that are detailed in conformity assessment modules. In terms of nonregulated products, ISO registration becomes a marketing decision dictated by customer-supplier quality requirements and the pressures imposed by the competition. Again, the marketing and competitive pressures for ISO registration vary from industry to industry.

As you read this book, you will discover that there are many questions about ISO 9000 that your company should ask. Are your particular products regulated by a specific EC directive? What are the specific customer requirements? Is the registrar qualified, recognized, or approved by the EC authorities or customer? The list of issues goes on. The important point is to focus on the issues surrounding ISO 9000 and conformity assessment.

Another important question to ask is: Are there other means to get my product into the EC? ISO 9000 registration is just one element in a broader set of conformity-assessment modules, or methods, that include product inspection, product testing, laboratory accreditation, and quality system registration/auditing.

WHAT IS CONFORMITY ASSESSMENT?

European Community laws, called *directives,* are driving the need for certifying quality systems and testing products. Depending on the product, the Europeans have established different means, called *modules,* for complying with an EC standard and for assessing conformance to standards. The different methods include:

Self-certification. Also called *manufacturer's declaration,* this is not being used as widely as anticipated. It is probably a matter of trust. Too many customers have been burned with false self-certifications. To remedy this, a self-certification may entail another type of conformity assessment, such as a product evaluation or quality systems audit. As well, EC national regulations insist that this method can't be used with regulated products. There is too much risk with regulated products, so regulatory authorities and customers want higher levels of assurance.

Product assessment. In this assessment, sample and/or representative products from a production run are tested and inspected to determine their conformance to customers' requirements. Engineering drawings and calculations may also be checked.

Quality system registration. In this assessment, the supplier is audited by an independent third party. For example, when the supplier passes the ISO 9000 audit, it is placed on a list that all customers can use to check certification levels. This is becoming the dominant form of conformity assessment. Companies want to minimize risk, especially with the growing tendency to increase the amount of products being outsourced. A small defective component can result in a catastrophic failure or a product recall.

HOW DO YOU COMPLY WITH THE STANDARDS?

In the U.S., a company complies through a third party, called a *registrar. The registrar is an independent body with knowledge, skills, and experience to evaluate a company's quality systems.* Registrars provide two basic services: they audit against one of the three ISO quality standards (ISO 9001, ISO 9002, or ISO 9003), and they place the company on a list of suppliers that have been certified by their auditors.

In a third-party assessment, a registrar evaluates an ISO 9000 applicant's quality systems. The applicant pays the registrar to conduct the audit and to place the applicant on the particular register. Quality system registration is sometimes called *quality system certification* in the U.S. and Europe.

The registrars also provide other services, such as quality manual evaluation, preassessment, and consultations. Unfortunately, these peripheral services, however structured by the registrar, can present an appearance of conflict of interest.

Before going further, several important terms should be clarified. *Certification* or *registration* is considered the all-encompassing term for registering quality systems. *Product certification* is primarily the process of conducting a product assessment. In this book, certification and registration are synonymous. When referring to product assessment, we'll refer to it as product certification. As well, the terms *assessment/audit* and *assessor/auditor* are often used interchangeably.

WHO EVALUATES REGISTRARS?

Registrars are approved and certified by accreditors. In the U.S., the Registrar Accreditation Board (RAB) is a private accreditor of registrars. It's common for U.S. registrars to be cross-certified or accredited by a European accreditor, or to have a working relationship that is spelled out in a Memorandum of Understanding (MOU). Accreditors are often approved and certified by national bodies or federal agencies.

The U.S. government has proposed establishing a vertical structure consisting of a recognition body, accreditors, and registrars. This is known as the Federal Conformity Assessment Systems Evaluation (CASE) program. The program, probably voluntary, would allow for federal government agencies to oversee and accredit registrars in regulated areas dealing with specific products and/or services, such as the Food and Drug Administration with medical devices and the Consumer Product Safety Commission with toys.

SHOULD YOU PURSUE REGISTRATION?

This is the fundamental question that every company considering registration should answer. There is no simple answer. However, the following discussion may clarify some of the surrounding issues and help your decision.

Regulated products, customer requirements, and competitive pressures will usually force a company and its suppliers to seek registration. National requirements may also compel a company to become registered.

ISO 9000 is becoming accepted by a number of large U.S. companies, many of whom are requiring ISO 9000 certification as a condition of business. It is either replacing or supplementing existing supplier quality requirements.

There are two major perspectives to address when considering registration, the external and internal. The external questions examine how registration improves your market position, perception, and profitability. *The basic external questions are:*

1. *Do you design, manufacture, or distribute a regulated product?*

2. *What do your customers or customers' customers require?*

3. *What is your competition doing?*

Internal issues surrounding whether or not registration is pursued are:

1. *Does ISO 9000 improve efficiency, effectiveness, or the economy of the organization?*

2. *Is coordination, cooperation, or communication improved?*

3. *Are internal customers and/or stakeholders involved with ISO implementation?*

DOES A SMALL COMPANY HAVE TO BE REGISTERED?

Does a small company, especially one that's two or more tiers away from the customer requiring registration, have to be registered? If you supply regulated products that deal with health, safety, environmental, or consumer issues, you will very likely have to follow and comply with the same procedures as those of larger firms. For example, the EC requires some form of conformity assessment of highly regulated sector products, including natural gas appliances, toys, and safety equipment. For other products, certification depends on customer requirements. This is a general answer. The costs of certification are not small and may be considered a required cost of doing business in the EC.

In general, your customers or customers' customers will dictate whether your company should be registered. It often is a requirement to sell products in certain markets. It may be an internal decision of balancing risks and controls. Or the decision may be based on perceived need. ISO certification can instill trust with customers, or it can be used as a sales inducement. There is no doubt that ISO registration is more difficult for a small supplier that doesn't already have engineering, production, information, or quality process documentation. So, it's important for smaller companies to evaluate the issues surrounding registration, including customer requirements, type of product, type of processes, risk, cost of failure, internal controls, level of internal quality, and history of operations.

HOW DO YOU SELECT A REGISTRAR?

Carefully. In a nutshell, you should look for:

Good chemistry between the registrar and your company. Can you work and partner with the registrar? Does the registrar understand your needs, and can they be fulfilled over the long term?

Background, reputation, and credibility. Has the registrar successfully certified companies in your industry? If so, talk to these companies.

Competence and reliability. Is the registrar accredited or certified by the Registrar Accreditation Board (RAB) and preferably by one or more European accreditors?

Cost and value. Is the cost of one registrar's certification competitive with others? Can and do you want the registrar to offer other services that add value to your organization or help promote competitiveness?

ARE ALL REGISTRARS CREATED EQUAL?

No. The basic issue is credibility and trust. Who accredits and certifies the registrar? Has it been done by a credible European or U.S. accreditor? *Is the accreditor a "notified body," or one that has been cleared and qualified by a national certification agency?* In the future most, if not all, registrars of regulated products will be certified by a government agency or national authority.

HOW LONG DOES REGISTRATION TAKE?

If you already have a quality initiative in place, and it has been working properly for a number of years, registration may take as little as six months to a year once the auditors have started. If a company doesn't have a quality program or instead has a cosmetic program—one where quality posters, messages, and process-control charts are used to convince auditors and customers of a quality commitment—then registration may take two years or more. On average, it probably takes about a year to a year and a half to become registered once the commitment has been made.

A major problem is that some registrars are so booked that the wait, the queue, may be as long as six months or more just to schedule a preassessment audit. The preassessment audit reviews the quality documentation and the quality manual to ensure that the basics of the quality standard are addressed. So, start the documentation and the quality systems development before the auditor's preassessment.

HOW MUCH DOES REGISTRATION COST?

Cost is based on many factors, including number of sites, number of product lines, location, size of facility, number of employees, level of registration pursued, level of existing quality program, types of services required, types of consulting services required, and so forth.

In 1990 the Registrar Accreditation Board conducted an informal survey of several registrars based on the following criteria:

- single site

- single product line

- two hundred to three hundred employees

- registration to ISO 9002

- first attempt successful registration

- no corrective action or post-assessments

The direct costs to the company seeking registration ranged from $10,000 to $15,000, plus expenses. Expenses involved travel, food, and lodging. If you want dual registration (a domestic registrar and a European registrar), add about $4,000. If your company requires consulting, surveillance, or other types of assessment services, costs can rise significantly. Also note that internal costs are not included and can be significant.

Registration costs also have gone up recently due to the rising demand by companies seeking registration. It is a simple matter of supply and demand. Demand for registration is higher than the supply of registrars and auditors. The result is that total costs are rising substantially.

WHAT TO DO IF YOU HAVE ANOTHER TYPE OF QUALITY PROGRAM

Many companies already are complying with other quality standards, such as Ford's Q101, GM's Targets of Excellence, or the U.S. military's MIL-Q 9858A. What should be done if your customer requires compliance to a new quality certification, ISO 9000?

There are two options available: (1) create separate but parallel quality systems using ISO 9000 as a model or (2) review existing quality systems and harmonize them to ISO 9000 standards.

The first option is not preferable in many operations. It creates redundant paperwork, controls, and, inevitably, confusion. The second option is being considered more and more as companies realize that ISO 9000 may become the global quality standard. *Even while the existing quality systems may be superior in terms of addressing continuous improvement, product innovation, and customer satisfaction, the foundation quality systems and documents should be ISO 9000–based.* In this option, existing quality documentation is kept and modified to reflect ISO 9000 requirements. This option makes sense for the many organizations that have already invested time, effort, training, and other resources to comply with other quality criteria.

The choice is up to your organization, costs, constraints, customer requirements, competitors' pursuits, and your company's improvement initiatives.

How Do ISO 9000 Requirements Relate to the Malcolm Baldrige National Quality Award?

The Malcolm Baldrige National Quality Award (MBNQA) is a prize acknowledging world-class quality performance in the areas of customer satisfaction, human resource management, quality planning, and quality metrics, among others. The award is given yearly to a maximum of two companies in each of three categories, which include manufacturing, small business, and service organizations. In contrast ISO 9001, ISO 9002, and ISO 9003 are a means to certify and register suppliers in basic quality systems criteria.

In general, while there are differences between the approach and content of these two models, they shouldn't create conflicts for an organization. It is usually assumed that ISO is a useful first step on the journey to the MBNQA.

There are similarities between the two, but there are also significant differences, as indicated by the sidebar on the facing page.

Benefits of Registration

Les Schnoll, Dow Corning's ISO Program and Quality Auditing manager, listed ten benefits of registration:

1. Customers are more receptive to implementing a supplier partnering relationship with companies with whom they have developed well-defined and mutually agreed-upon requirements. This can result in a significant competitive advantage to the registered supplier of products or services.

2. A prevention attitude can be implemented throughout the company, accompanied by early detection and corrective action systems, providing evidence not only of a quality management system but of positive quality attitudes and management's commitment to continuous improvement.

3. Clear, well-documented procedures are established and maintained.

Similarities and Differences Between the Malcolm Baldrige National Quality Award and ISO 9000	
MBNQA	*ISO 9000*
U.S.–based	Globally applicable
Highest level of quality	Highest common-denominator quality criteria
"World-class" quality	Doable and attainable quality
Advanced TQM award	First step in the TQM journey
Systems-oriented	Systems-oriented
Broad quality criteria covered	ISO 9001 generically covers Baldrige criteria
Focus on control, participation, and improvement	Focus on control
Exclusive, only two winners per category	Inclusive, all can become registered
Quality criteria higher and more demanding, stressing customer satisfaction, quantifiable results, and continuous improvement	Quality criteria generic; customer satisfaction and continuous improvement not emphasized

4. Adequate quality training is available for all members of the organization.

5. There is a greater emphasis to focus on the needs of the customer.

6. Registration enhances the ability to compete in world markets.

7. There is a reduction in the number of costly and time-consuming customer audits.

8. There is evidence of compliance with a set of non-biased criteria by an independent third party, indicating an adequate level of assurance of an existing quality system.

9. Customers purchasing products from registered organizations benefit from the ability to reduce the level of costly and time-consuming incoming inspection and testing of supplied products. Compliance with the criteria of an international quality standard, coupled with the willingness of the supplier to provide its customers with product certification, should indicate an adequate level of assurance of product quality and consistency.

10. There is enhanced marketability through the use of a recognizable logo and inclusion in a registered suppliers listing.

WHAT ARE CONSTRAINTS AND DISADVANTAGES TO REGISTRATION?

ISO 9000 quality systems registration is no panacea. It involves costs, risks, and uncertainty. As well, there is still much confusion among countries about the acceptance of registrars. The following are additional constraints and disadvantages of registration:

- Europeans are providing mixed signals and mixed messages about recognition of third countries' (those outside of the European Community) conformity assessment.

- U.S. governmental agencies, accreditors, and registrars can provide diverse views and opinions on ISO 9000.

- Registration sometimes follows a herd mentality.

- Consultants warning that ISO registration is necessary for all products create incorrect and mixed signals.

- There is poor understanding about the nature of European directives requiring registration.

- Auditor and registrar quality vary.

- ISO 9000 is not universally accepted.

- Interpretation of ISO and other standards is inconsistent.

- ISO 9000 has different levels of certification, and companies don't know which to pursue.

- Registration is expensive.

In general, confusion reigns over the conformity assessment process at the accreditor and international levels. In the certification community, there are lots of conflicting messages. Accreditation bodies, registrars, auditors, and companies are all trying to understand and cope with global business and certification. The result is that many companies are procrastinating pursuing registration until EC and U.S. uncertainties are resolved.

WHAT HAPPENS IF YOU DON'T PURSUE REGISTRATION?

An important element of the competitive marketplace is continuous improvement. The ISO committee chartered to develop the standards, Technical Committee 176, will update ISO 9001/9002/9003 every four years. Also, the committee is developing guideline documents that are presently optional. These are "should" guidelines for companies implementing specific quality systems in such areas as software or process materials. However, these "should" guidelines also serve as early warning requirement documents. It may be only a matter of time until the "should" guidelines are incorporated into one of the "shall" standards; that is, ISO 9001/9002/9003. The goal by the year 2000 is to develop an integrated series of Total Quality Management systems standards that will encompass every element of an organization.

If the momentum continues through the 1990s and more countries adopt ISO 9000 or its equivalent standards, ISO 9000 will truly become global and a condition of business and trade at intra- and intertrading bloc levels.

Some companies may resist pursuing registration, perhaps because they are from newly developing or East bloc countries and don't have the national certification structure, money, or resources to become certified. What happens to these companies if ISO registration is required by everyone? It's an intriguing thought. It may develop that we end up having a two-tiered international supplier base—those companies with continuously evolving quality systems and those with static or no quality systems at all.

HOW DO YOU OBTAIN INFORMATION OR INFLUENCE EC LEGISLATION?

If you design or market products or services globally, how do you obtain information or influence the standards-development process? Keep current with the changing standards that can impact your firm. For example, you may find your products have just been barred from entering a market through a simple stroke of a pen. You say, "I wasn't told." Well, "That's tough" is probably the response you'll hear.

For small and medium-size U.S. firms doing international business, I strongly recommend belonging to and participating in industry trade groups. Most regulated and unregulated product trade groups have retained high-level, knowledgeable managers who are responsible for tracking international standards and conformity assessment regulations.

The following are ways to have your voice heard or to find more information:

- subscribe to EC or standardization newsletters

- contact ANSI and participate in the appropriate working group

- contact the National Center for Standards and Certification Information (NCSCI) to obtain standards information or to track regulations affecting your product

WHERE DO I GO FROM HERE?

Semi-facetiously, the first thing you should do is buy this book, read it, and discuss it with your customers and employees. Then examine and determine the following:

- What do your customers and/or stakeholders want?

- What is your competition doing?

- If you use ISO 9000 and/or pursue registration, what are the internal benefits?

If you want more information, contact the organizations listed in the Resources section. You can also attend an ISO seminar or possibly retain a consultant. The ISO seminar will tell you if you must be certified and inform you of the latest developments, and the consultant will assist you in implementation, certification, and Total Quality Management. Once you have followed each step, you will have a good idea if registration is right for you. An important caveat is in order: The process is not inexpensive. Pursue ISO 9000 only if it adds value to your business and to your customers.

How Is This Book Organized?

This book follows a vertical structure, starting with global competitiveness and ending with specific recommendations for pursuing and achieving registration. The following describes what is found in the chapters of *ISO 9000*.

Chapter 1: Introducing ISO 9000: Questions and Answers. Harmonization and standardization have been the province of technocrats and economists. Specialized concepts and language have evolved around these subjects. These concepts are introduced and the most pressing ISO 9000 questions are answered.

Chapter 2: The Global Competition Game. The global marketplace and competitive pressures are encouraging the development of free trade areas such as the EC and the North American Free Trade Agreement (NAFTA). Within and across these trading blocs, there is a need for product transparency and quality assurance.

Chapter 3: Global Standardization. Standards are a symbol of a nation's economic development. At the heart of the international acceptance of ISO 9000 is the desire to enhance trade through compatible process and product standards. In an integrated and interdependent global economy, ISO 9000 and similar technical standards have become tools for furthering national political/ economic agendas and improving a company's competitiveness.

Chapter 4: ISO 9000 Series Quality Systems Standards. ISO 9000 is a mechanism for ensuring that products conform to technical requirements. ISO 9000 is divided into two parts. ISO 9001/9002/9003, as customer-supplier documents, are characterized by "shall" instructions. ISO 9004 and other ISO 9000 documents are internal documents and are characterized by "should" recommendations.

Chapter 5: EC Conformity Assessment. Global harmonization and conformity assessment are being driven by the Europeans. The EC wants to enhance the competitiveness of its companies as well as preserve its citizen's quality of life. To obtain this assurance, the EC is promoting international testing and certification, of which ISO 9000 is a part.

Chapter 6: U.S. Conformity Assessment. U.S. government and private conformity assessment activities are exploding. The U.S., among other industrialized nations, is developing a voluntary vertical certification structure consisting of nation-to-nation mutual recognition agreements of test results, accreditation of testing bodies, and registration of companies.

Chapter 7: Registrars and Quality Auditing. Accreditors certify testing bodies, laboratories, and registrars. Registrars audit and certify companies. The accreditation and registration structure is being duplicated in most major industrialized countries.

Chapter 8: How to Become Registered. This may be the most valuable chapter of the book. The entire registration process is explained from a company's perspective.

Chapter 9: Successful Registration: The White-Rodgers Story. White-Rodgers (W-R), an Emerson Electric division, was the first U.S. company in the gas industry to become ISO registered. Its insights, challenges, and responses are important to all companies seeking registration.

Chapter 10: ISO 9000: Decision Point. ISO registration comes down to a basic business question: What's in it for me? It involves balancing benefits and costs. Only if benefits exceed costs should registration be pursued.

CHAPTER 2

The Global Competition Game

Are we going to be a services power? The double-cheeseburger-hold-the-mayo king of the whole world?

—Lee Iacocca

There seems to be universal agreement that times are tough. The global as well as the U.S. economy is stale bordering on stagnant. The current trade imbalance is high. Jobs, jobs, and jobs are the major public-policy issue of the decade. *Global trade and product consumption are seen as mechanisms to spur high-wage employment growth.*

In this chapter, we'll explore the issues of quality and standardization in the context of global trade and competitiveness. Both topics will help explain the burgeoning interest in ISO 9000 and other globally accepted mechanisms that promote growth, generate jobs, and accelerate the integration of the world's economies.

INTRODUCTION TO COMPETITIVENESS

The Cold War is over and the Japanese won.
—PAUL TSONGAS, U.S. Senator

Essentially, ISO 9000 is about competitiveness—how companies regain, ensure, and improve it. Before we go any further, let's clarify what we mean by competitiveness at the national level and the company level.

GLOBAL COMPETITION: THE NEW U.S. REALITY?

I don't meet the competition. I crush it.
—CHARLES REVSON, Chairman,
Revlon

In June 1983, President Reagan established the President's Commission on Industrial Competitiveness. The commission was charged with identifying ways to improve the private sector's ability to compete in world markets. The issue was studied, a series of reports was issued, and little was subsequently accomplished.

The reasons vary. Times were flush and few cared about economic competitiveness. Consumer spending, which constitutes two-thirds of the U.S. economy, was at an all-time high. Military-sector job creation was churning along due largely to stratospheric deficit spending. As well, there were basic philosophical objections to dealing with economic competitiveness. Reagan appointees did not subscribe to industrial or central planning, largely because of the communist central planning failures. Republican administrations preferred a laissez-faire approach in which market signals dictated actions. Why would anyone care about commercial competitiveness? Times were good and they were just going to get better.

However, as the saying goes, What goes up . . . well, you know the rest. The bubble burst. Things changed. This is now the decade of retrenchment and introspection. Communism is near dead. Military readiness must evolve to commercial preparedness. Global commercial competition is torrid. Deficits inhibit government action. Unemployment is high. High-paying quality jobs are scarce.

In this context, the commission's 1985 report is prescient. It stated: "America's competitive preeminence in world commerce has eroded over the past decade. We are being challenged in the trading arena by our European trading partners and industrializing nations in Asia and Latin America. Sustaining America's competitiveness is important for maintaining our standard of living, our foreign aims, and our national security."[1]

WHAT IS COMPETITIVENESS?

> *It is ridiculous to call this an industry. This is rat eat rat, dog eat dog. I'll kill 'em and I'm going to kill 'em before they kill me. You're talking about the American way of survival of the fittest.*
> —RAY KROC, Founder of McDonald's

Little was accomplished as a result of the report. It was ahead of its time. In this country, and probably in others, nothing in the public sector is accomplished until there is a fundamental need or urgency. And this has to be viscerally understood by a large sector of the population so it is reflected in public-opinion polls. These serve as the mandate for action in a democracy. The U.S. is now at this point. Times are tough. Action is required.

One thing the report accomplished was to define the critical elements of a nation's competitiveness: "Competitiveness for a nation is the degree to which it can, under free and fair market conditions, produce goods and services that meet the test of international markets while simultaneously maintaining and expanding the real incomes of its citizens. *Competitiveness is the basis for a nation's standard of living.* It is also fundamental to the expansion of employment opportunities and a nation's ability to meet its international obligations."[2]

Similarly, a company was defined as competitive if "*it can produce products or services of superior quality or lower costs than its domestic and international competitors.* Competitiveness is then synonymous with a firm's long-run profit performance and its ability to compensate its employees and provide superior returns to its owners."[3]

WHAT IS QUALITY?

As quality has become more customer-focused, customer-based definitions, such as "anticipating and exceeding customer expectations," are operationalized into terms that are useful to those who design and/or manufacture products as

---

[1] President's Commission on Industrial Competitiveness. January 1985. *Global Competition: The New Reality* (Washington, D.C.: Superintendent of Documents), Vol. 2, p. ix.

[2] Ibid., p. 6.

[3] Ibid.

well as to those who deliver services. Without these operational quality definitions, there is little chance that market- or customer-based quality definitions will be realized. Therefore, a widely accepted ISO operational definition of quality—"ability to satisfy stated or implied needs"—is more realistic and usable. For most companies, these requirements are usually detailed in some form of standard, which may include drawings, policies, procedures, and instructions.

EUROPEAN ECONOMIC CHALLENGES

World trade means competition from anywhere; advancing technology encourages cross-industry competitors.
> —MARY ANN ALLISON, Vice President, CitiCorp

The explosion of interest in ISO 9000 can be understood in terms of the early fears of a competitiveness deficit that fostered the development of the EC. The purpose for forming the EC was to remove all trade barriers that inhibited the free movement of people, money, goods, and services thereby creating business opportunities that would enhance everyone's quality of life. A single market would create economies of scale, optimize the use of resources, create opportunities for industrial specialization, and enhance the ability of EC firms to compete globally.

Bruce Millan, a member of the European Commission, expressed the competitive challenge: "Now that the frontiers are coming down, competition is going to get fiercer. A company in Andalusia (Spain) is not just going to measure up to competitors in Galicia (Spain) or Asturias (Spain), but also much more than before to French, Dutch, or German firms, not to mention the fiercer competition from outside the Community."[4]

THE EARLY FEAR OF "EUROSCLEROSIS"

In the 1970s "Eurosclerosis" was a popular European rallying cry. There was double-digit inflation and high unemployment in Europe. There was omnipres-

---

[4] *Opening Up the Internal Market.* Commission of the European Communities. Brussels, Belgium. 1992, p. 28.

ent fear that U.S. companies would use Europe as a third-world supplier of cheap labor, a dumping ground for waste, and a captive market of eager buyers. The Americaphobes also feared the loss of quality-of-life conditions, including culture, environment, consumer-product safety, and health.

I remember visiting Europe in the early 1960s and seeing examples of American cultural and economic omnipresence. Europeans were adopting many American words into their languages—the French deridingly calling it Franglais. Billboards on every street shouted the product virtues of Ford, IBM, and Marlboro. It's interesting that while American culture currently still seems influential, the dominant billboard and product presence seem to be touting Japanese and Pacific Rim firms.

Just as many books in the U.S. warn on the impending economic war with Japan, many European best-selling books in the '70s and '80s warned of U.S. economic incursions, the resulting chaos, and portending third-world life-styles. A common theme of these books was the perceived high-technology and product-development gaps between European and U.S. companies.

While European products sold well overseas and had high perceived quality, they often did not incorporate the latest technical developments and were costly to manufacture. In general, the Europeans prided themselves on quality in terms of dedication and attention to detail, which may have worked well for individual products but did not transfer well to highly technical, mass-produced items.

During this time, the definition of quality was also evolving to incorporate technical elements such as reliability, maintainability, aesthetics, and durability. These quality attributes were directly influenced by rapidly advancing engineering and manufacturing capabilities.

In the 1980s and 1990s, the Europeans, perceiving the U.S. a waning economic power, shifted their concern and fear to the Japanese. European consumers marveled at and purchased steady streams of innovative high-quality Japanese consumer products, while European industrialists and technocrats were increasingly concerned with these low-cost industrial products.

WHAT CAUSED THE COMPETITIVENESS PROBLEM?

What were the causes of the EC's competitiveness problem? Poor economic performance was caused by poor management, inadequate technologies, poor commercial quality systems, conflicting technical standards, inadequate testing/

certification laboratories, adversarial labor relations, and nonproductive government policies.

In terms of developing highly technical products, the problems were exacerbated. Different technical requirements among countries made even development of simple consumer products difficult. Each European nation developed technical standards to protect its markets and industries.

Technical differences were replicated in many products, which formed de facto market barriers. To illustrate, a traveler in Europe would have to carry multiple electrical wall adapters for his or her personal products. Product development became crazy. Also, the Europeans did not have a major presence in many cutting-edge technologies such as integrated circuits, biotechnology, aerospace, and telecommunications.

NEW CONCEPTS GAIN CURRENCY

In the EC, telecommunications symbolizes many of these challenges. For example, Spain has a three-second busy tone while Denmark has a two-second busy tone; France's telephone numbers are seven digits while Italy's can be any length; and Germany's phones operate on sixty volts while others operate on eight volts. In this context, telecommunication concepts like interoperability and harmonization become especially significant since they impacted economic competitiveness and military preparedness.[5]

In the essential telecommunications market, it was critical to establish common standards so data could be shared across the continent without additional, expensive equipment. New words—*transparency, interoperability, compatibility, standardization,* and *harmonization*—gained wide currency. It was recognized that to establish a common market there must be harmonized technical standards and commonly accepted methods of ensuring conformance to these standards.

Of the 279 directives initially promulgated, more than half dealt with technical product standards. In targeted industries involving the environment, safety, health, and consumer products, the EC adopted international standards or developed common product standards. They also identified measures and test methods to be used to ensure conformance. ISO 9000 is an example of one of the international conformance standards that was adopted.

[5] George Yip, *Total Global Strategy* (Englewood Cliffs, NJ: Prentice Hall, 1992), p. 55.

Trade Barriers Survey

To solicit EC industry perspectives on trade barriers, a survey was sent to more than twenty thousand companies of the twelve EC-member states. The survey confirmed what the EC bureaucrats believed: the number-one barrier to trade was technical standards and regulations.° The following barriers were most often cited as barriers to trade:

1. Technical standards and
   regulations

2. Administrative barriers

   } Approximately equal in survey

3. Frontier formalities

4. Freight transport regulations

5. Value-added tax references

6. Capital market control

7. Government procurement
   restrictions

8. Implementation of Community
   Law

} Approximately equal in survey

° H. Gundlach, "The Role of the Accreditation and the Route to the CE Mark." Raad voor de Certificate, Driebergen, Holland. August 1991.

FORMATION OF A COMMON MARKET

The solution to the challenge of improving competitiveness was to accelerate the economic integration of Europe. A common internal market with open borders would improve product quality, create jobs, improve competitiveness, and enhance everyone's quality of life.

Timing for the formation of a common market was propitious, its union accelerated by:

- dissolution of the Soviet Empire

- high-density population

- common social and cultural history

- common borders and geography

- wide concern for health, safety, and environmental issues

Twelve nations formed the European Community. The twelve EC nations are Belgium, Denmark, France, Germany, Greece, Ireland, Italy, Luxembourg, the Netherlands, Portugal, Spain, and the United Kingdom. Individually, these countries were influential and powerful. As a united community, they would have the potential to exert tremendous economic power. The European market would be the single largest market in the world—340 million compared to 250 million Americans and 125 million Japanese. EC living standards were already among the highest in the world.

In terms of a trade area, the European Free Trade Association (EFTA) also adopted many of the technical standards of the European Community. EFTA consists of Austria, Finland, Iceland, Liechtenstein, Norway, Sweden, and Switzerland. And on May 2, 1992, the twelve EC and seven EFTA ministers signed a treaty to create a nineteen-nation free-trade zone, the European Economic Area (EEA). The EEA extends the EC single-market effort to the EFTA countries, including the four critical freedoms—the free movement of goods, capital, services, and labor. The EEA treaty incorporates many EC directives, regulations, and administrative decisions that the EFTA countries must adopt in order to participate in the single market.[6]

EUROPEAN COMMUNITY COMPETITIVENESS

A competitive world has two possibilities for you. You can lose or, if you want to win, you can change.
— LESTER THUROW, Economist

The formation of a common market was initially conceived as a government and business partnership. An important mission of the formation of the EC union was to create stable, high-wage employment for Europeans. It was up to busi-

---

[6] M. Treinen, "European Economic Area: Extends the EC's Single Market Across Western Europe," *Europe Now: A Report*. Washington, D.C. July/August 1992, p. 7.

nesses to design and manufacture high-quality products efficiently and economically. And it was up to the government, in this case the European Commission, to "frame an industrial policy that will provide an open and competitive business environment, including the legal, financial, and technical instruments to make it easier for businesses to develop partnership strategies."[7]

Jacques Delors, the president of the European Commission, expressed it this way: "It is above all at the Community level that, in the face of international competition, the public authorities can act to encourage productivity, mobilize resources on a large scale, organize long-term cooperation projects—to create, in other words, an environment which helps European businesses to enhance their competitiveness."[8]

EUROPEAN COMPANY COMPETITIVENESS

Industry in the Community can enhance its competitiveness by reducing the time taken to apply the results of fundamental research.
—EUROPEAN COMMISSION

The Europeans highly respected the U.S. and Japanese companies that treated the world, and particularly Europe, as one big market. European firms yearned to do the same, to quickly develop aesthetic, low-cost, high-quality products and services that could be tailored for specific markets in terms of quality, reliability, fit, function, detailing, instructions, and packaging.

Ford and GM were two successful models of this in Europe. They had well-established design, manufacturing, distribution, and marketing networks that optimized the distinctive advantages and assets of a country or region.

With economic integration, why couldn't European firms do the same with companies within its borders to capitalize on their distinct "world-class" abilities? Italy was known for its product design. The UK had good mechanical engineering resources. The Netherlands had state-of-the-art software and electronics facilities and engineers. The Germans had a worldwide reputation for manufacturing quality and attention to detail. The goal became to identify growing or

---

[7] *Increasing Industrial Competitiveness.* Pamphlet of the Office of Official Publications of the European Communities. Brussels, Belgium. 1992, p. 1.

[8] Ibid., p. 2.

emerging markets and pool the best EC resources to develop and deliver high-quality marketable products. These issues could only be decided by a coherent and comprehensive industrial policy based on a public-private partnership.

GOVERNMENT AND BUSINESS PARTNERING

> *We do not intend to create an economic area without ensuring that the healthy effect of competition is complemented by a greater degree of cooperation and solidarity.*[9]
>
> —JACQUES DELORS, President of the
> EC Commission

If the EC could identify companies or anticipate industries that would be critical to future economic development or would enhance the quality of life, then it would invest in these projects. The goal was to identify and encourage companies that could be competitive with those of Japan and the U.S. For example, one industry identified as critical to global competitiveness was commercial aviation, so a consortium of European countries subsidized Airbus. How successful have these direct investment projects been? It's still too early to tell. However, early indications seem to confirm that joint government and industry partnering is synergistic and could serve as a model for similar ventures in the U.S.

Europe's multinational firms, Philips Electronics of Netherlands and Daimler-Benz of Germany, are already partnering with their national governments and with the EC to develop new standards, manufacturing processes, and quality systems. All of which are essential components of the 1990s global competitive game.

These loose coalitions with national governments are mutually beneficial. The companies secure access to technology, markets, distribution, and finances. The national governments secure high-paying jobs. These firms are also forming partnerships with U.S. and Japanese firms to promote their corporate interests.

European businesses are learning from the Japanese how to play the global business game of capturing market share at the same time as protecting domestic industries from foreign incursions. Protected industries are different across the EC. It may be the automotive industry in Italy, farming industry in France, and fishing industry in Denmark. These are and increasingly will be the trade disputes and competitive battles of the 1990s.

---

[9] Ibid., p. 1.

LESSONS FOR THE U.S.

The European approach to competitiveness may have some lessons for the U.S. Traditionally, the U.S. has relied on market signals to provide the inducements to business growth. Laissez-faire economics prevailed over industrial planning. However, this approach contrasts with much of the world. Notably, the European and Japanese governments are cooperating with business to maintain high levels of highly paid employment as well as develop high-quality cost-competitive products and services.

In a recent publication, the Commission of the European Community expressed the intent and purpose of joint government-private cooperation and coordination:

> In the long term, the creation of stable jobs and prosperity in Europe will depend on strong and healthy businesses. That is why improving industrial competitiveness is one of the objectives of the European Community. The Community-wide single market gives businesses enough room to develop two of their major assets—their efficiency and the quality of their products. Within the single market—the world's biggest—it is primarily up to businesses themselves to devise ways of producing and selling better. Joint ventures and other forms of business cooperation can help. Meanwhile, the European Community is in the process of framing an industrial policy that will provide an open and competitive business environment, including the legal, financial, and technical instruments to make it easier for businesses to develop partnership strategies.[10]

HUTCHINS'S RULES OF GLOBAL BUSINESS

> *Anyone who believes that the competitive spirit in America is dead has never been in a supermarket when the cashier opens another checkout line.*
>
> —ANN LANDERS

For years, U.S. companies dominated world markets by being internally integrated. As I once wrote: "Conventional wisdom said that if a company owned the sources of raw material, processed the raw material, designed the products,

---

[10] Ibid.

machined, fabricated, marketed, and finally distributed the product, profits and market share would be assured. Vertical integration offered the advantages of standardization of products; control of operating, marketing, and distribution channels; and size and cost efficiencies."[11]

This could be seen in the auto industry where automakers controlled the entire design, manufacturing, distribution, and marketing process. Little was purchased and almost everything related to developing an automobile was performed in-house. It was believed that if a company owned the sources of raw material, designed the product, and controlled the mechanisms for selling, distributing, and servicing the product, the company could control product quality, service, and costs.

However, these assumptions become moot in a disaggregated global economy where individual customers want customized products and services, not me-too global products. George Yip, a widely written professor on global management, says: "The idea of a fully standardized global product that is identical all over the world is a near myth that has caused great confusion."[12] True global products or services can only be achieved by standardizing the core product and customizing its peripheral elements, such as product color or service. To produce and sell products in small niched markets requires a new philosophy based on entrepreneurship, global sourcing, and world-class, low-cost quality.

BUSINESS RULES

Recently, a professional group asked me to distill the rules of global business into a twenty-minute talk. Half in jest and half seriously, I said, "Sure, why not!" I gave it a shot and facetiously titled it "Hutchins's Rules of Global Business in the 1990s." The major points were:

1. Please your stakeholders

2. Do what you do best

3. Outsource all other work to "world-class" suppliers

4. Acquire processes and systems as well as products

[11] G. Hutchins, *Purchasing Strategies for Total Quality* (Homewood, IL: Business One Irwin, 1992), p. 15.

[12] G. Yip, *Total Global Strategy* (Englewood Cliffs, NJ: Prentice Hall, 1992), p. 55.

5. Judge "world-class" suppliers by quality, cost, and service

6. Innovate and improve continuously

Let's explore each one.

Please Your Stakeholders

> *The consumer is not a moron. She is your wife.*
> —DAVID OGILVY, Advertising Guru

Since Tom Peters wrote his opus *In Search of Excellence*, pleasing the customer has been a conventional wisdom of excellent business management. The customer was first considered the external customer, the final user; then the concept was enlarged to include the internal customer, the person next in line using one's products.

However, *the customer is only one of a growing number of stakeholders that must be satisfied in a global economy*. A customer may also be local authorities, state government, or federal government. More and more, regulatory authorities, dealing with safety, environmental, consumer, and health issues, are growing in importance. Therefore, a partial list of stakeholders would include final and internal customers, management and employees, shareholders, government, suppliers, and unions.

As the 1990s business universe becomes more inclusive, satisfying if not pleasing these stakeholders will become more important. It almost may be said that any one of these stakeholders may have the power of veto for a company to enter new markets, be profitable, or even survive.

Do What You Do Best

A company can't be all things to all people. An organization must focus on what it does best. *In a competitive economy, the goal is to become "world class," the best in one's market.* Best can be in terms of designing widgets, supplying typing services, washing cars, providing legal work, or assembling printed circuit boards.

As large companies attempted to please customers with a large variety of products, several problems arose. Products would have different features, performance, or external aesthetics. Large plants would be built with parallel management, design, production, marketing, and distribution systems. Overlapping systems created redundancies that inevitably resulted in confusion. Bureaucracies were built that tended to protect turf instead of focusing on pleasing the customer.

As well, no company ultimately has the ability to be the best in each area. This requires an abundance of resources that no organization has. What often occurs is that resources are spread too thin and the organization does many things only moderately well.

Outsource All Other Work to "World-Class" Suppliers

Vertical integration is losing its appeal to new forms of cooperation, coordination, and communication. Global competition, high product-development costs, high-quality expectations, low-cost expectations, shortened product life cycles, and individual customer requirements are accelerating the change to partnering. More often, work is sourced to a single and/or acceptable alternate supplier.

Many Japanese companies form *keiretsus,* formal or informal financial, engineering, manufacturing, and supplier networks. While still new in the U.S., these relationships are characterized by close product development and business relationships. Cost, design, delivery, customer service, and other usually proprietary information is commonly shared. The hoped-for results are minimizing redundancies, enhancing communication, and improving coordination.

Supplier-partners are expected to be very good at what they do; in other words, to be "world class." Implicit in the partnering arrangement is that the customer selects one or two supplier-partners for each product line. The rationale for two suppliers is that one supplier may not be induced to change quickly, to continuously improve and innovate, and to continuously lower costs. As well, the customer assumes inordinate risk with one supplier in terms of an act of God, strike, or other unforeseen event stopping shipments.

Often, supplier-partners are nimble entrepreneurs that have knowledge of local customer requirements and access to global information, can adapt quickly to new market messages, and are monomaniacal in the pursuit of pleasing the customer. These small organizations are usually not inhibited by bureaucratic resistance or inertia. Flexibility, quickness, and action are the code words for their success.

Acquire Processes and Systems As Well As Products

Many purchasing professionals still focus on buying products instead of focusing on securing reliable supplier processes and systems. This requires a shift of thinking, moving upstream to focus on the systems that design, manufacture, and deliver products instead of the results, the products.

Modern quality management assumes that if customer requirements are understood and internalized, then the supplier has upstream quality systems and processes in place to address these requirements. If these processes are controlled and improved, then there is some assurance that the products and services coming out of these are defect-free. A major element of ISO 9000 is to ensure quality systems exist and quality documentation supports the quality initiative.

Judge "World-Class" Suppliers by Quality, Cost, and Service

How is "world class" determined? Traditionally, commercial buy decisions were based on price, availability, and delivery. Similarly, consumer buy decisions were largely based on price and packaging. *Now, consumer and commercial buy decisions are more complex, based on verifiable quality, total cost, eye-catching design, environmental friendliness, and other factors.*

While consumer decisions are often the result of on-the-spot visceral responses, both consumer and commercial buy decisions are based on well thought-out, researched decisions. Often, the consumer will defer to the independent evaluations conducted by *Consumer Reports* or similar publications. To obtain verifiable confirmation and assurance of compliance to standards, commercial buy decisions are based on quality audits, self-certifications, product, testing, or inspection.

In the U.S., EC, and Pacific Rim, conformity assessment mechanisms, such as third-party auditing, are widely used to ensure quality in commercial and public contracting. In the EC, Siemens, the German electronics giant, requires third-party confirmation to ISO 9000 in 50 percent of its customer-supplier contracts and is encouraging its other suppliers to pursue compliance.[13]

---

[13] "Want EC Business? You have Two Choices," *Business Week,* October 19, 1992, p. 58.

Innovate and Improve Continuously

> *The productivity and competitive problems American manufacturers*
> *face result from ineffective top management—petrified in place,*
> *unwilling to accept change, failing to provide vision and leadership.*
> —PHILIP ALSPACH, President, Intercon

Standing still in a fast-moving economic stream is the equivalent of moving backwards. Treading water is death in hi-tech markets. The obvious solution is to innovate and improve continuously. Innovation is the ability to conceptualize and commercialize new products. Improvement is the ability to control process and system variation so there are no defective products.

Deming's Purchasing Philosophy

W. Edwards Deming's philosophy of defining targets and minimizing variation also applies to purchasing and sourcing. He believes that multiple machines, instructions, personnel, methods, or supervisors could cause unwanted variation, which he calls *assignable-cause variation*. He postulates that a process in control has all of its major causes of variation identified, monitored, measured, controlled, and minimized.

The purchasing process could result in unnecessary and unwanted variation if a customer has multiple suppliers of the same product. The customer has to communicate the same information to all suppliers. A supplier could possibly misinterpret this information, resulting in additional sources of variation or nonuniform quality products.

INTERNATIONAL-LEVEL PLAYING FIELD OF SUPPLIERS

Partnering takes several forms. It may be a relationship in which the customer doesn't inspect products, but insists on independent evidence or verification that certain quality systems exist and critical manufacturing processes are controlled. Or partnering may mean that the supplier becomes integrated into the customer's product-development effort, from product concept to design, manufacturing, testing, packaging, and disposal.

Higher levels of customer-supplier integration require more standardization, harmonization, and compatibility. In very close partnering, the supplier is almost an extension (some call it captive) of the customer. The supplier has similar design, manufacturing and quality systems, procedures, and processes. Even communications are computerized using similar systems and protocols. The closeness of the customer and key suppliers extends to just-in-time production, common communications networks, joint product development, and other forms of integration.

How does a customer ensure communication and understanding with suppliers many miles away? Suppliers come in many forms and abilities. The challenge is to create an international-level playing field of suppliers. *The assumption is that if companies adopt an internationally accepted quality standard such as ISO 9000 and are assessed in compliance to this standard, they have the minimum requisite quality systems and processes.* While the standard may not indicate "world-class" quality, it does indicate a minimum level of acceptability, a first hurdle in the continuous quality-improvement journey.

Implicit in this is that the international language of trade is quality-based. Suppliers speaking this language can show compliance through an independent third party and are placed on a register available to companies throughout the world. This system of placing suppliers on registers indicating levels of quality compliance will continue through the next ten years. If the system succeeds, ISO 9000 registration may well be a condition of business in many industry sectors. Registration will become part of the contractual boilerplate for bidding projects. And the world's supplier base potentially could consist of companies that have complied with internationally approved standards, such as ISO 9000, and those who haven't, resulting in a globally tiered supplier base.

HIGHER QUALITY LEVELS

Customers pay only for what is of use to them and gives them value.
Nothing else constitutes quality.
—PETER DRUCKER, Management Expert

Purchasing and the customer-supplier relationship has radically changed in the last ten years. (See the sidebar on page 39.) An important element of this change is the emphasis on higher levels of quality. Quality has evolved through these stages:

1. Incoming material inspection

2. Quality systems

3. Statistical quality control

4. "World-class" quality[14]

INCOMING MATERIAL INSPECTION

Product inspection, a conformity assessment mechanism, is the identification, measurement, or testing of critical or major product characteristics. It may be simple or complex. For example, product inspection may be dimensional-, physical-, chemical-, or performance-based; may involve visual, mechanical, or electrical testing; may be destructive or nondestructive; may be sophisticated or a yes/no testing; may assess 100 percent or just essential product characteristics; or may evaluate 100 percent or a statistical sample of the products in a population.

The problem with product inspection is that it occurs after the fact. The product may be accepted, scrapped, used as is, or reworked. And since inspection may be random and statistical, products could still be nonconforming if the process was not stopped and the cause of nonconformance not eliminated. Inspection does not identify and eliminate the cause of the problem and is not prevention-oriented.

Besides being wasteful, inaccurate, impractical, and risky, worst of all, inspection sends the wrong messages to internal and external suppliers that mistakes are accepted. This is unacceptable in a very competitive global economy.

QUALITY SYSTEMS

> *One accurate measurement is worth a thousand expert opinions.*
> —GRACE HOPPER, U.S. Navy Admiral

In 1959 the Department of Defense issued a quality standard, MIL-Q 9858A, that eventually became the basis for many subsequent quality standards, such as ISO 9000 quality systems standards. (The table of contents of MIL-Q 9858A and

---

[14] These concepts were developed and evolved in my National Association of Purchasing Management (NAPM) seminars, and were introduced in *Purchasing Strategies for Total Quality* (Homewood, IL: Business One Irwin, 1992), pp. 48–62.

Changing Nature of Customer-Supplier Relations

Old Approach	New Approach
Purchasing is a tactical issue.	Purchasing is a strategic issue.
Price is a major factor in buy decisions.	Quality is equal to price in buy decisions.
Front-end price is important.	Life cycle costs are critical.
Quality is conformance to specifications.	Quality is broadly defined, mainly in terms of the customer.
Quality is satisfying customer requirements.	Quality is anticipating and exceeding customer requirements.
Purchasing is a cost area.	Purchasing is a profit/loss area.
Manager supervises functions.	Corporate officers lead functions.
Products are simple.	Products are complex.
Buyer or agent purchases products.	Single supplier-partner provides products.
Defects are accepted.	Zero defects are expected.
Material quality is measured in terms of defect levels.	Material and service quality is measured in many ways.
Inspection is used to control defects.	Prevention is used to eliminate defects.
Quality is static.	Quality throughout organization and supplier base continuously improves.
Supplier is simply selected.	Suppliers are continuously monitored and evaluated.
Design, manufacturing, and purchasing are static.	Design, manufacturing, and purchasing are flexible.
Communication is paper-based.	Communication is electronically driven.
Product life cycle is long.	Product life cycle is short.
Delivery can be at any time.	Delivery is just-in-time to specific loading dock.

Source: G. Hutchins, *Purchasing Strategies for Total Quality* (Homewood, IL: Business One Irwin, 1992).

ANSI/ASQC ISO 9001-1987 are shown in the sidebars on pages 41–43.) During the intervening years, MIL-Q 9858A became the internal and external quality standard of choice and the benchmark quality standard in the regulated, non-regulated, military, and commercial sectors. In the regulated area, the Food and Drug Administration (FDA) customized its Good Manufacturing Practices (GMP) quality program for medical-device manufacturers and pharmaceutical firms. The Environmental Protection Agency (EPA) and the Nuclear Regulatory Commission (NRC) developed their own standards around MIL-Q, which also served as the basis for their quality audits. Commercial companies also did the same. These early efforts migrated overseas where MIL-Q evolved into national European standards and the North Atlantic Treaty Organization (NATO) AQAP 1 quality standard.

"Womb to Tomb" Quality

ISO 9000 evolved from MIL-Q 9858A and still retains much of its flavor, purpose, and perspective. ISO 9000 is certainly not cutting-edge quality. It is a document that a technical committee hammered out through consensus, and represents attainable quality systems for many businesses.

The MIL-Q standard emphasized documented internal quality systems and procedures. The notion, also applied to ISO 9000, is that "womb to tomb" quality was fully documented. The problem was that quality systems may be in place and operating properly. However, the quality systems and operations may not be producing aesthetic, low-cost quality products and services that please the customer. As can be seen from MIL-Q 9858A Quality Requirements shown in the sidebar, this standard does not address final customer satisfaction, internal customer satisfaction, quality metrics, quality planning, prevention, innovation, or continuous improvement. As well, current management tools and techniques such as benchmarking, process control, quality function deployment, and others are also not addressed.

STATISTICAL QUALITY CONTROL (SQC)

> *In quality control, you are controlling the downside.*
> —HAROLD GENEEN, Chairman, ITT

The next step in the customer-supplier relationship was statistically based prevention and improvement. SQC originated in the early 1980s in the commercial sector, in companies such as Xerox, Motorola, Ford, and IBM.

MIL-Q 9858A Quality Requirements

1.   Scope

1.1 Applicability

1.2 Contractual Intent

1.3 Summary

1.4 Relation to Other Contract Requirements

1.5 MIL-I 45208

2.   Superseding, Supplementation, and Ordering

2.1 Applicable Documents

2.2 Amendments and Revisions

2.3 Ordering Government Documents

3.   Quality Program Management

3.1 Organization

3.2 Initial Quality Planning

3.3 Work Instructions

3.4 Records

3.5 Corrective Action

3.6 Costs Related to Quality

4.   Facilities and Standards

4.1 Drawings, Documentation, and Changes

4.2 Measuring and Testing Equipment

4.3 Production Tooling

4.4 Use of Contractor's Inspection Equipment

4.5 Advanced Metrology Requirements

5.   Control of Purchases

(continued on the following page)

MIL-Q 9858A Quality Requirements (*continued*)

5.1 Responsibility

5.2 Purchasing Data

6.   Manufacturing Control

6.1 Materials and Materials Processing

6.2 Production Processing and Fabrication

6.3 Completed Item

6.4 Handling, Storage, and Delivery

6.5 Nonconforming Material

6.6 Statistical Quality Control and Analysis

6.7 Indication and Inspection Status

7.   Coordinated Government/Contractor Actions

7.1 Government Inspection at Subcontractor or Vendor Facilities

7.2 Government Property

8.   Notes

8.1 Intended Notes

8.2 Exemptions

Motorola's trademarked 6 Sigma program is an example. It attempts to define standards of operational excellence and strives to achieve no more than 3.4 defects per million operations around defined targets. This prevention-driven philosophy became one of the main impetuses for continuously measuring improvement and setting competitive benchmarks.

Not all companies have adopted this warrior pursuit of excellence and improvement. Usually, companies in rapidly evolving environments, such as high technology, strive for this high level of quality. It is difficult and requires everyone's single focus in the united goals of customer satisfaction, prevention, measurement of all activities, quantum leap innovation, company/supplier–wide continuous improvement, and market share.

ANSI/ASQC ISO 9001–1987

0.0   Introduction

1.0   Scope and Field of Application

2.0   References

3.0   Definitions

4.0   Quality System Requirements

4.1   Management Responsibility

4.2   Quality System

4.3   Contract Review

4.4   Design Control

4.5   Document Control

4.6   Purchasing

4.7   Purchaser Supplied Product

4.8   Product Identification and Traceability

4.9   Process Control

4.10 Inspection and Testing

4.11 Inspection, Measuring, and Test Equipment

4.12 Inspection and Test Status

4.13 Control of Nonconforming Product

4.14 Corrective Action

4.15 Handling, Storage, Packaging, and Delivery

4.16 Quality Records

4.17 Internal Quality Audits

4.18 Training

4.19 Servicing

4.20 Statistical Techniques

"World-Class" Quality

> *In quality management, you are controlling the upside.*
> —Greg Hutchins

The Malcolm Baldrige National Quality Award in the U.S. and the European Quality Award in Western Europe have become international awards for quality excellence.

Malcolm Baldrige National Quality Award

In just a few years MBNQA has become the preeminent U.S. business trophy. However, it has lost some of its luster and cachet as recent winners have experienced economic lapses like Chapter Eleven, weak financial returns, lost market share, and collapsing quality reputations.

Much, perhaps too much, has been written and promised about the merits of the award. Regardless, "for the few and the proud" the Baldrige journey is the apex of U.S. quality achievement. Several years ago, some companies (notably Motorola) started asking suppliers to work toward the award and be assessed. More large companies similarly have assessed their suppliers to Baldrige criteria.

Malcolm Baldrige National Quality Award

The seven major sections and the maximum points for each section are shown below.

Section	Maximum Points
Leadership	95
Information and Analysis	75
Strategic Quality Planning	60
Human Resource Development and Management	150
Management of Process Quality	140
Quality and Operational Results	180
Customer Focus and Satisfacation	300
	1000

However, problems arise when companies still at the inspection level of quality are evaluated to "world class" standards. Many U.S. suppliers have not been exposed and do not think in terms of global criteria and benchmarks. This is about to change.

European Quality Award

The European Quality Award, first presented in 1992, follows the spirit of the MBNQA. The EQA is annually presented to one company in Western Europe that demonstrates the most successful pursuit of Total Quality Management. European Quality Prizes may be awarded yearly to several companies that demonstrate quality excellence and the pursuit of continuous improvement.

The EQA is divided into two equal parts, Enablers and Results. The Results criteria deal with what a company has achieved and is achieving. The Enablers

---

European Quality Award Criteria

Enablers	Points (in percentages)
Leadership	10
People Management	9
Policy and Strategy	8
Resources	9
Processes	14
	50%
Results	
People Satisfaction	9
Customer Satisfaction	20
Impact on Society	6
Business Results	15
	50%

Source: "The European Quality Award—Application Brochure" (Eindhoven, The Netherlands: The European Foundation for Quality Management, 1993), pp. 1–10.

criteria deal with how results are being achieved. The rationale for the inter-relationships among the nine award criteria is as follows: "CUSTOMER SATIS-FACTION, PEOPLE [employees] SATISFACTION, and IMPACT ON SO-CIETY are achieved through LEADERSHIP, driving POLICY AND STRATEGY, PEOPLE MANAGEMENT, RESOURCES, and PROCESSES, leading ultimately to excellence in BUSINESS RESULTS."[15]

The evolution of the MBNQA and EQA can be best understood in the context of global standardization and the pursuit of competitiveness which are discussed in the next chapter.

---

[15] "The European Quality Award—Application Brochure" (Eindhoven, The Netherlands: The European Foundation for Quality Management, 1993), p. 10.

CHAPTER 3

Global Standardization

*The Lord told Noah: "Make thee an ark from gopher wood sealing it
with pitch."*

—THE BIBLE: GENESIS

Standards have been used for years to communicate requirements, establish
common units of measurement, facilitate interchangeability and interoperability,
enhance product reliability, and simplify products.

The Assyrians, Mayans, Aztecs, Egyptians, Greeks, and Romans used standards to construct temples, boats, and aqueducts, many of which still exist today.
The secret of these early developments was a common and consistent method, or
standard, for design construction and measurement. Standards were also developed to assure and enhance productivity.

Standards have been a basic element of society's economic and technological
development for years. *The development and acceptance of international standards will play an important role in the 1990s in global trade, national competitiveness, and a company's profitability.*

BASIC CONCEPTS AND PRINCIPLES

What we've got here is a failure to communicate.
                                        —STROTHER MARTIN, *Cool Hand Luke*

First, let's define what is meant by the term *standard*. The National Standards Policy Advisory Committee defines a standard as: "A prescribed set of rules, conditions, or requirements concerning definitions of terms; classification of components; specifications of materials, performance, or operations; delineation of procedures; or measurement of quantity and quality in describing materials, products, systems, services, and practices."[1]

A major element is the emphasis on a prescribed and accepted set of rules. These rules are often developed in areas that deal with public safety and health. This trend started in the nineteenth century when fire, boiler, and fastener standards were developed to prevent catastrophic failures (boiler explosions, for example, devastated entire towns and resulted in thousands of deaths) and to preserve the well-being of society.

In this century, consumer safety and environmental issues have similarly come into the spotlight. Chernobyl, Three Mile Island, ozone depletion, the *Challenger* disaster, food carcinogens, and product failures have frightened people and prompted government surveillance and regulation. Serving the public interest has long served as justification for stronger government involvement and intervention.

STANDARD AS A COMMUNICATIONS TOOL

Aside from safety and health reasons, technical standards also serve other important purposes such as:

- improving product and process quality

- reducing product liability and litigation

- communicating requirements to stakeholders

- establishing common objectives

[1] "What Is . . . a Standard?" (New York: The USA Standards Institute), p. 1.

- communicating complex information in a simple, structured manner

- promoting compatible methods for testing products

- standardizing parts for production

Standardization of parts is especially important for maintaining product integrity. When a part is designed, there is often a long, iterative process to ensure that it can be manufactured. This process becomes more complicated when parts are purchased from distant suppliers whose quality is difficult to monitor. Therefore, engineers attempt to enhance existing products or design new products using existing components. In this way, design iterations are minimized.

Different types of standards such as policies, procedures, and drawings are also a means to communicate needs and requirements. Engineering drawings communicate requirements to internal manufacturing and to external suppliers. Policies communicate a corporate direction and purpose. Procedures communicate approved or suggested forms of behavior.

TECHNICAL STANDARDS—LANGUAGE OF GLOBAL TRADE

Technical standards have become part of the language of global trade. General Agreement on Tariffs and Trade (GATT) signatories have pledged to ensure that "technical regulations and standards are not prepared, adopted, or applied with a view to creating obstacles to international trade."

The GATT Standards Code was later incorporated into the U.S. Trade Agreements Act of 1970, which state that federal agencies under the Act are required to

- not engage in standards activities that are prepared, adopted or applied to create, or have the effect of creating, unnecessary obstacles to the foreign trade of the U.S.;

- ensure that imported products are treated no less favorably than domestic products;

- use international standards, if appropriate, as a base for developing new standards;

- develop standards based on performance rather than design criteria, if appropriate; and

- allow foreign suppliers access to their certification systems on the same basis as access is permitted to domestic suppliers.[2]

STANDARDS—TOOLS FOR DEVELOPMENT OR FOR PROTECTION

It is clichéd to say that the world has become smaller and homogenized. No one knows how trade will look in the near future, whether it will be free trade, managed trade, or trade war.

Many countries presently restrict the movement of products through tariffs and technical barriers. A government imposes a tariff or a duty on specific products usually to give domestic producers some equity or advantage.

On the other hand, a national specification can become a non-tariff technical barrier, specifying the type of material, dimensions, physical properties, chemical properties, performance, or other product characteristics. A technical specification may also define the required processes with which a manufacturer must comply before securing approval to sell its products in a certain country.

U.S., European, and International Standards Organizations

In ISO 9000 certification, several standards-related groups have a direct impact on standardization. The following list of U.S. and international professional and standards-related organizations figure prominently in the harmonization of technical standards:

- ANSI
- ASQC
- RAB
- NIST

- ISO
- IEC
- CEN/CENELEC
- ETSI

ANSI

American National Standards Institute, a private-sector organization, coordinates much of the voluntary standards development in the U.S. ANSI represents the U.S. in various international standards bodies.

---

[2] U.S. Department of Commerce, International Trade Administration, *The Tokyo Round Agreements: Technical Barriers to Trade*. Vol. 4. Washington, D.C., September 1981.

U.S., European, and International Standards Organizations (*continued*)

ASQC

American Society for Quality Control is a U.S.-based association of more than one hundred thousand quality-management and -assurance professionals. ASQC actively promotes U.S. quality activities. For example, it manages the Malcolm Baldrige National Quality Award, administers the U.S. Technical Advisory Group (TAG) to ISO Technical Committee 176, and established the Registrar Accreditation Board (RAB).

RAB

Registrar Accreditation Board was established for the purpose of certifying registrars and quality auditors. These auditors conduct ISO 9000 audits.

NIST

National Institute of Standards and Technology is a U.S. government agency in the Department of Commerce. It formerly was known as the National Bureau of Standards (NBS). Among its functions are overseeing the Malcolm Baldrige National Quality Award and laboratory certification efforts.

ISO

International Organization for Standardization consists of ninety-one national standards organizations. The U.S. signatory is ANSI. ISO serves as an international forum for discussing, developing, and coordinating global standards. The International Organization for Standardization has issued more than six thousand standards, probably the greatest number of any international standards group.*

(*continued on the following page*)

---

* M. Breitenberg, *The ABC's of Standards-Related Activities in the United States* (Washington, D.C.: Superintendent of Documents), May 1991, p. 2.

U.S., European, and International Standards Organizations (*continued*)

IEC

International Electrotechnical Committee is the electrical equivalent of ISO. The ISO and the IEC together have developed more than 85 percent of the world's standards. To give an idea of their size, there are more than three thousand ISO/IEC working groups.

CEN/CENELEC

European Committee for Standardization (CEN) promotes European standards in non-electrotechnical areas. European Committee for Electrotechnical Standardization (CENELEC) develops European standards in the electrotechnical areas. They were formed in 1965 and are nonprofit, international standards-making bodies. Their members are the sixteen nations consisting of the twelve European Community nations as well as four European Free Trade Area nations. Their goals are to develop European regional standards in place of national standards.

CEN/CENELEC advises the EC Commission on harmonizing technical standards within the EC and EFTA. These European norm technical standards are prefixed by an *EN*; EN 29000 is equivalent to ISO 9000, for example.

ETSI

European Telecommunications Standards Institute was formed in 1988 to accelerate the development of the high-priority telecommunications standards. The European Commission would first issue a broad directive stating the need for a standard in a particular area and then assign CEN/CENELEC/ETSI to define the technical specifics.[*]

[*] Office of Technology Assessment, *Global Standards: Building Blocks for the Future* (Washington, D.C.: Superintendent of Documents), 1992, p. 71.

U.S. STANDARDS DEVELOPMENT

They (the Japanese) recruit their managers from the factory floor. We get ours out of law school.
                                                        —JOHN GIBBONS

Today, approximately four hundred U.S. standards-making organizations have developed and adopted more than thirty thousand voluntary standards. This number does not include federal, state, and city procurement specifications, codes, rules, and other regulations.[3] These groups include trade associations, professional societies, general-membership organizations, third-party certifiers, and consortia of standards developers.[4]

U.S. government standards involvement has traditionally focused on areas of safety, health, environment, consumer protection, and in general, areas that affect public welfare. For example, the U.S. has seen a tremendous increase in Occupational Safety and Health Administration (OSHA), Food and Drug Administration (FDA), and Environmental Protection Agency (EPA) regulations.

To a large extent, U.S. standards development reflected our cultural and political biases. It was private, voluntary, consensus-driven, and bottom up. U.S. standards development also had a strong market, user focus. Standards were developed by subject matter experts and employees of organizations that wanted to input a standard's development. Once developed, it was up to prospective users to determine whether they wanted to adopt the standard. The goal of U.S. standards activity was to develop consensual standards that would be widely understood, adopted, and used.

Sometimes, a voluntary standard became part of a national regulation or became a de facto world standard because it represented the state of the art or was widely adopted. For example, probably the most recognized and adopted standard is the American Society of Mechanical Engineers (ASME) code for pressure vessels and boilers.[5]

U.S. standards development in the last one hundred years was managed by

[3] M. Breitenberg, *The ABC's of Standards-Related Activities in the United States* (Washington, D.C.: Superintendent of Documents), May 1991, p. 1.

[4] Office of Technology Assessment, *Global Standards: Building Blocks for the Future* (Washington, D.C.: Superintendent of Documents), 1992, pp. 49–51.

[5] A. Batik, *The Engineering Standards: A Most Useful Tool* (Ashland, OH: Book Master/El Rancho, 1992), p. 15.

technocrats. *These U.S. standards-making efforts usually represented the state of the art so the rest of the world reluctantly or happily adopted them and designed products consistent with the U.S. standards.* A certain technical hubris evolved. It essentially said: We have the technology and we want you, the world, to design around it. Product development by fiat antagonized many. But in the last ten years, the U.S. has found the tables reversed; its input and control of international standards are seriously hampered by past approaches and unilateral practices as others want to develop their own technical standards with little input from the U.S.

HIGHEST OR LOWEST COMMON DENOMINATOR QUALITY STANDARD

A camel is a horse that was designed by a committee.
—ANONYMOUS

Consensus among standards stakeholders has been the key concept driving U.S. and EC standards development. Consensus is reached when most of the concerned individuals agree on the major issues and good-faith efforts have been made to resolve differences. I have seen international standards meetings try to resolve one major objection among sixty or more committee members. Obviously, consensus decisions take more time and patience to develop accepted positions that become international standards.

As a practical matter, how does Technical Committee 176, the ISO committee assigned for developing and updating ISO 9000, establish consensus? Is it a matter of majority or unanimity or somewhere in between? And, is it on all issues or on critical issues? And then, what is a critical issue?

These are questions that ISO TC 176 must address. And as such, points to the heart of the process's advantages and problems. The standard is the work of an international committee that tries to assuage many different political, economic, and technical constituencies. As such, some consider it as the highest or the lowest common denominator quality standard.

Challenges to Global Standardization

An economic conundrum is that the northern-hemisphere countries have well-developing economies and technologies while southern-hemisphere countries, for the most part, are less or underdeveloped. This disparity has caused problems in international political, technical, and environmental conferences. The equitable

Challenges to Global Standardization (*continued*)

development and implementation of technical standards is an area that will require more sensitivity by the national delegates from the more-developed nations. Otherwise, the newly or less-developed countries will be reluctant to adopt international standards such as ISO 9000.

Dr. Horacio Martirena, an independent Argentine ISO consultant and a TC 176 member, sees the following challenges or impediments to global standardization:

ISO 9000 is ostensibly a global standard. But is that really true! The following factors endanger the "global" character of the standard:

- control of TC 176 secretariats
- economic and motivation factors deter participation
- language difficulties during discussions
- language problems during translations
- different levels of technical development

It is very important to have as many countries as possible participating in the standardization activities. Developed countries such as the U.S., the UK, Canada, France, Germany, and Holland hold most of the TC 176 secretariats and convenorships.

A large number of other developed and nondeveloped countries do not have a strong influence on the TC 176 standardization activities. This may be due to two reasons: (1) personal expenses incurred during traveling and attending all the meetings are high, and (2) it still seems unclear to many delegates what global standardization means.

TC 176 carries out its work in English prior to issuing the final standard. Only at the last step are documents translated into French or Russian. The language used during most of the committee work is not, in most cases, familiar to all delegates. This places a considerable strain on non-English-speaking delegates.

Translation of the final standard into local languages is performed by people who did not participate in the TC 176 discussions, and, therefore, do not know the "flavor" of each paragraph or sentence. Local translations may not accurately reflect the idea behind each ISO requirement of the original English version.

The large differences in technical and economic development among countries of the world also make the application of, or the incorporation on a day-to-day basis of, "state-of-the-art" technical standards difficult. It may have to be considered that a 100 percent updated technical global standard could result as an unintended noneconomic barrier to trade.°

°Source: Personal communication

ANSI/ASQC Consensus Criteria

ANSI and ASQC have adopted the following criteria for developing consensus on the U.S. Technical Advisory Group (TAG) to ISO Technical Committee 176. These criteria are also similar to the international consensus criteria:

1. All substantial concerned parties have had the opportunity to express views concerning the proposed standard, and these views have been considered.

2. Evidence of use or potential use of the proposed standard is available.

3. There is no recognized "significant" conflict with another standard. If there is, the conflict has been resolved.

4. Other related national and accepted standards have been considered and evaluated.

5. The standard's benefits are aligned with the public interest.

6. No unfair provisions have been included.

7. The standard is scientifically and technically accurate.

8. All consensual issues have been resolved.

CONFLICT AMONG U.S. STANDARDS ORGANIZATIONS

Standards development is a survival issue to some U.S. standards-making and -related organizations. ANSI is the self-designated U.S. national standards development organization in ISO. ANSI is also the self-designated official U.S. national standards organization. It's interesting to talk with members of the U.S. standards community about this. ANSI's status is not fully accepted by other major U.S. players, and some in the international standards community voice the same concern. Major U.S. standards groups, in particular the American Society for Testing Materials (ASTM), the American Society of Mechanical Engineers (ASME), and the Institute of Electrical and Electronic Engineers (IEEE), are sometimes not willing to cooperate, coordinate, or defer to ANSI. It is estimated that only approximately eighty-five hundred or 25 percent of all nongovernmental standards have been screened and approved by ANSI.[6]

---

[6] Office of Technology Assessment, *Global Standards: Building Blocks for the Future* (Washington, D.C.: Superintendent of Documents), 1992, p. 53.

ASTM's position, also reflected by other U.S. standards-related organizations, is that: "ASTM would become solely a feeder of U.S. consensus standards and positions into ANSI for blessing as U.S. 'National' standards and into ISO for blessing as 'International Standards.' And, ASTM might not even be able to play that limited role. If Europe and the U.S. agreed to develop and require the use of ISO standards in their respective markets, sales of ASTM standards, nationally, and internationally, might be so eroded that ASTM could no longer support itself."[7]

COMPETITIVE IMPORTANCE OF STANDARDS

We were fairly arrogant, until we realized the Japanese were selling quality products for what it cost us to make them.
—PAUL ALLAIRE, CEO, Xerox

The voluntary consensus process of standards development has worked remarkably well for a long time. However, in a highly competitive global economy problems arise. The U.S. doesn't dominate the world in key design and manufacturing innovations. And the U.S. can't impose its view on the rest of the world. Regional trading blocs, such as the EC, are developing their own standards that favor indigenous national companies. Technology is advancing faster than the consensus driven process can accommodate.[8] The problems with voluntary consensual standards are becoming a major trade and competitiveness issue.

In a recent report, the Office of Technology Assessment (OTA), an investigative arm of the U.S. Congress, stated that "among the dangers that the United States faces today is a loss of competitiveness, due partially to a failure at leadership in the international standards development process."[9]

Leadership and consensus is not coming out of the U.S. standards development community, so this is being used as a rationale for U.S. government involvement through the National Institute of Standards and Technology (NIST) and other federal agencies.

The OTA put the standards issue in the middle of the competitiveness debate. The OTA was charged to determine to what extent U.S. standards developments

[7] Ibid., p. 23.
[8] Ibid., p. 1.
[9] Ibid., p. 49.

support the growth and competitiveness of the U.S. economy in a rapidly changing global environment. The results were disturbing and challenging. OTA concluded that:

- Standards help determine the efficiency and effectiveness of the economy; the cost, quality, and availability of products and services; and the state of the nation's health, safety, and quality of life.

- *In an information-based global economy, standards are employed strategically as marketing tools and also to interconnect economic activities.*

- U.S. voluntary consensus standards development process is not working because of a lack of cooperation and trust.

- *Failure to bring American standards-setting organizations together and to work out their relationship with the government is a very serious problem in dealing with other nations in a world where economic welfare through economic warfare are dominant policy issues.*

- Paralleling the lack of unity in the private-sector standards community is a lack of coordination and policy making at the federal level.

- U.S. government has tended to disregard or underestimate other government's efforts to use standards as a means to expand business, create market opportunities, or enhance trade opportunities.

- Due process of accounting for all stakeholder views will become a global issue because of the rapid advance of technology, shift to a global economy, the rise of user groups, and government involvement.[10]

Why did OTA recommend these changes? One major reason was to form and develop the rationale for more government involvement in the development·of technical standards that would position the U.S. more favorably vis-à-vis the EC and the Japanese.

---

[10] Ibid., pp. 1–20.

EC STANDARDS DEVELOPMENT

ISO will be a must for any company in Europe.
—WINFRIED WERNER,
ITT Semiconductors, Germany

The Europeans are no longer concerned with their military security. They now want to determine their own economic destiny. They understand the importance of technical standards, including ISO 9000, as being critical to forming a common economic market and to competitive success. Most of the EC's initial 279 directives or laws dealt with technical product and process standardization issues. The standards were used as a means to harmonize different national requirements and as a major tool for economic and technical unification.

LEVELING OUT THE PLAYING FIELD

Economists, politicians, and others complain that when their country's products cannot enter a certain market, the playing field is not level. This metaphor is often apt. U.S. companies doing overseas business confront special or unusual marketing, manufacturing, design, safety, performance, labeling, or packaging standards just as foreign producers find similar requirements in the U.S. Many U.S. and EC industries and companies have developed standards that are technically biased in their own favor.

The U.S. and other major countries have used standards to position themselves in new markets. In the last forty years, the U.S. has been the world's largest market. If offshore producers wanted to sell products in the U.S., they were expected to use U.S. technology and follow U.S. standards. Now, tables are turned. The EC is the world's largest market, and the EC is expecting countries to accommodate to its standards. In fairness, the Europeans are saying they will adopt or defer to international standards as much as possible. However, this has become a bone of technical and economic contention. The Europeans perceive that U.S. companies are whining about the need to level the playing field. To lessen these tensions, countries on both sides of the Atlantic are trying to adopt international standards and to find acceptable means to assure their conformance.[11]

U.S. companies are concerned that the EC will not allow American experts

[11] C. Dawson and J. Lewelling, "Level Play Fields: International Standards, Product Certification, and the Global Marketplace," *Regulation*, Summer 1991, pp. 25–29.

access to CEN/CENELEC standards development. Standards may be used to deny or impede access to the European market. Recently, the U.S. government has requested a voice in the EC standards-setting and -developing process. The problem is that third country governments are not permitted to review and comment on early drafts of a technical standard. Consensus on the broad scope and direction of the standard is reached early while details are fine-tuned later. Thus, it is difficult to introduce changes once the development process starts.

From the European perspective, standards-setting bodies perform public functions that affect the health and welfare of its citizens. The EC Commission, unlike the U.S., funds standards development and implementation primarily in regulated industrial sectors. And many European national standards organizations are government supported as shown below.

The Europeans also dominate the international standards groups. EC countries administer more than 70 percent of the ISO technical committee secretariats. As well, they dominate the regional standards groups, such as CEN/CENELEC, which third countries can't actively participate with but can have only observer status. With this influence, EC officials can graciously defer to or accept ISO standards since European nations manage most of the ISO committee's work.

European Standards Organizations

Country	Standards	Status	Staff	Number of CEN Secretariats*	Annual Output of Standards
Germany	DIN	2	596	34	1,400
Denmark	DS	1	65	6	250
Spain	Aenor	1	70	0	850
France	Afnor	1	446	17	1,100
Italy	UNI	1	48	3	270
Netherlands	NNI	2	100	2	110
United Kingdom	BSi	1	1,200	10	660

Status:

1. Organization under private law but given a public-service function by the state

2. Private organizations

* These 7 countries accounted for 70 out of 82 technical committees in 1987.

Source: F. Nicolas and J. Repussard, *Common Standards for Enterprises* (Luxembourg: Official Publications for the European Communities, 1988), p. 26.

EUROPEAN AEROSPACE QUALITY

One major success story of Western European private-public partnering has been in the European aerospace industry, particularly with Airbus. A major element of the success story is having aerospace industry suppliers comply with ISO 9000 standards.

IMPORTANCE OF QUALITY TO AEROSPACE

First a little background may help. The EC aerospace industry employs nearly half a million people in design, manufacturing, servicing, and other areas. There are three major industry customer groups: civil aviation, military aviation, and space programs. All three emphasize quality. According to Ingo Herbst, the vice president of the European Aerospace Contractors Association (AECMA), quality is a prerequisite for national and international competitiveness: "Customer satisfaction is the prerequisite for lasting success of companies in national and international competition. . . . The customer gets product/service which is suitable for the intended purpose and which fulfills his expectations. Quality of products and service cover all phases within their life span, which means that it starts early in the project and ends when scrapping the product."[12]

STRUCTURE OF EUROPEAN AEROSPACE

There are thirty-five to forty aerospace companies that design and manufacture in the EC. The supplier base of these companies ranges from between five hundred to ten thousand suppliers. To evaluate, qualify, certify, and monitor each supplier by each aerospace company would be redundant and costly. The solution was to develop a system of uniform standards and a common means to evaluate them. This is a common problem as well in U.S. industry sectors where large companies use many of the same suppliers. Medical devices, telecommunications, automotive, and other large industry sectors are similarly developing uniform standards and common means of evaluating suppliers.

The Europeans developed the European Aerospace Supplier Evaluation

---

[12] I. Herbst in a talk for the European Organization for Testing and Certification (EOTC), "The European Aerospace Quality Scene," *Testing and Certification in Europe* (Brussels, Belgium: EOTC, 1992), pp. 6–7.

(EASE) program more than twenty years ago. EASE publishes a register of suppliers for its members that includes thirteen hundred suppliers that have been approved to ISO 9000 or AQAP (NATO quality) standards. The audits are conducted by bodies that have been approved by national airworthiness authorities. The register has been very successful in reducing the number of audits.[13]

TECHNICAL HARMONIZATION

There are thousands of technical standards. Some are simple, others complex. Just about every product used or consumed in the world is defined in terms of form, fit, and function that are spelled out in technical standards. Assembly, subassembly, and component level requirements are similarly spelled out.

A technical document does not become a national or international standard until there is wide consensual agreement and subsequent use. The global adoption and implementation of ISO 9000 is an example of a process called *standardization* or *harmonization. Harmonization is the European term for creating community-wide, uniform technical rules for processes and products.* Harmonization attempts to make a standard transparent or compatible in terms of application and content. Harmonization is especially imperative with standards dealing with health, welfare, consumer protection, and environmental issues, and is often incorporated into law.

EC STANDARDS DEVELOPMENT

The EC wants to create a harmonized system of regional standards that replaces many existing national product standards. Many of the twelve member countries had followed different paths to develop standards and to ensure they were followed. The goal is to have a company comply with one European or international standard instead of each country's national standards. The EC calls its approach to standards development the *EC New Approach Directives.*

EC directives are not technical process and product standards. They are policy documents. Two approaches were initially pursued. One targeted regulated areas dealing with health, safety, consumer, and environmental products. The other

[13] Ibid.

approach targeted nonregulated products. The European Commission contracted with technical standards groups such as CEN, CENELEC, and ETSI to develop specific technical standards. In regulated industries, CEN and CENELEC are either developing standards or are adopting existing international standards. The latter approach obviously makes sense in order to avoid conflicting standards and duplication of effort.

Once standards have been written and harmonized, how does the European Community know that manufacturers and companies are complying with the standard and the directive? There must be a mechanism for checking and assuring conformity to standards and specifications. The mechanisms are called *conformity assessment* and include such means as quality system audits, product testing, or self-certification. This is a huge undertaking, with millions of potentially affected companies and tens of thousands of product-testing laboratories.

If this type of thinking is enlarged to encompass the world, a manufacturer will have to conform to only one globally accepted technical standard and be approved through a conformity assessment mechanism, which may include ISO 9000 quality systems audits. Just think of this as the ultimate in one-stop certification and testing.

FREE TRADE, MANAGED TRADE, OR TRADE WAR?

They all come back to the same thing: We have got to decide what free and fair trade is all about, and we've got to level the playing field to be competitive. These are the gut issues.
—LEE IACOCCA

Some U.S. critics speculate that the Europeans are being unfair and claim that the EC is hiding behind a wall of protection. They subsidize industries such as farming, aircraft, and computers. Free-traders scream "unfair" and assert the U.S. usually doesn't directly subsidize companies. The Europeans do, and Airbus is the notable European example.

What's the truth? Well, many countries subsidize or help their domestic companies compete. For example, the Japanese and Koreans assist their industries through incentives and by providing outright financial support. But it is very difficult to identify those industries and companies that will be the winners. There are often as many losers as winners in this process.

TODAY'S TRADE

Free trade has not worked for the U.S. Managed trade, or as some say, *mutually beneficial trade*, advocates say that free trade positioned our industries in unfair competition against low-wage countries. High-wage jobs are exported and low-cost, not necessarily high-quality, products are imported.

How did this pattern start? While trade disagreements more and more involve the EC, accusatory fingers were first pointed at the Japanese and Pacific Rim nations. Critics maintain the Japanese and others have used predatory practices such as selling goods below cost to secure markets. The laissez-faire economists proposed a trade quid pro quo: we'll open our markets if you open yours. With the benefit of hindsight, this has not worked. The Japanese government and industry groups seem to have targeted specific U.S. industries for incursion and takeover. The industries cover America's best, including steel, consumer electronics, auto, and the list goes on. Economist John Culbertson sums up the current angst well: "Japan managed its foreign trade to achieve its economic advance by gaining for itself the rewarding, skill-building, high-income, success-making industries of the times. . . . Through this one-sided 'trade,' Japan made a net takeover of desirable U.S. industries and jobs."[14]

This rhetoric will rise in the next several years, largely echoing Culbertson's bleak analysis: "Japan understood the foreign-trade game, played realistically to win, and won. The United States did not understand the game, based its action on a utopian crusade for a world governed by laissez-faire economics, and lost."[15]

TOMORROW'S TRADE

How will the world's economies look in ten years? No one really knows. One scenario foretells of three major global trading blocs, consisting of the European Community, North America, and the Pacific Rim. There will be (1) free trade, (2) managed trade, or (3) trade war. Laissez-faire economists hope for the first option. However, this is difficult in a world in which each country looks out for its own industries and constituencies. A trade war would probably put the world in a recession. The logical option is some form of managed trade comparable to that which presently exists. The near-future challenge is that the rising trading blocs may promote free trade within the bloc and manage inter-bloc trade.

[14] J. Culbertson, *The Trade Threat* (Madison, WI: 21st Century Press, 1989), pp. 3–4.
[15] Ibid., pp. 5–6.

THE USE OF TECHNICAL STANDARDS AS A TRADE BARRIER

Some economists see technical standards such as ISO 9000 as a potential non-tariff barrier to global free trade. In other words, countries and/or companies will require ISO registration as a condition of business. If all Europeans did this, then conceivably it could create a closed European market, a "Fortress Europe."

While conceivable, it is not realistic. About 25 percent of the EC gross domestic product is exported. If the EC develops trade barriers, then the U.S. and other trading regions would retaliate, resulting in a trade war. All governments are trying to avoid this and are downplaying this scenario because it's in everyone's interest to maintain free trade.

ISO 9000 is an international series of quality technical standards that many countries want to use to maintain the free flow of products. By adopting this international quality standard, a country could defuse the criticism that it isn't playing fair by trying to restrict entry of imported products.

CHAPTER 4

ISO 9000 Series
Quality Systems Standards

It costs a lot to build bad products.
—NORMAN AUGUSTINE, Chief Executive,
Martin Marietta

ISO 9000 evolved directly from a market need to obtain greater assurance that products conform to technical requirements. Customer requirements in commercial contracts are commonly spelled out in technical specifications. Typically, these detail such product factors as dimensions, materials, tests, performance, reliability, maintainability, durability, and so on.

A major problem with technical specifications is they don't guarantee customer's requirements are consistently met. If there are deficiencies in upstream systems, such as in design, manufacture, parts delivery, or even service specifications, the output of the systems, the products, may be deficient.

"HOW DO I KNOW THESE PRODUCTS CONFORM TO REQUIREMENTS?"

To secure assurance, the fundamental question a customer should ask is: *"How do I know supplied products comply with requirements?" The answer to the question can be broken down into two issues: (1) developing universally accepted technical and quality systems standards and (2) developing similarly accepted mechanisms for ensuring conformance to the standards.*

In terms of the first point, if quality system standards and guidelines could be developed to complement technical product or service requirements, then the customer would have a higher level of assurance that most products or services meet requirements.[1]

TRUST BUT VERIFY

> *What one sees depends upon where one sits.*
> —JAMES R. SCHLESINGER

Developing mechanisms for ensuring conformance to the standards would provide some assurance of the quality or consistency of the processes that produce the products or provide the services. *The rationale is if quality systems are in place, working properly, monitored, and controlled, then outputs, the products or services, should satisfy the customer.* This is the fundamental premise of modern quality control and the basis for most modern customer-supplier relationships.

There must be some mechanism for ensuring that standards are being followed; that is, some form of verification. Three types of verification are commonly used: self-certification, product certification and quality system registration. The first two alternatives can be redundant, unreliable, and costly; they are also product- and inspection-based.

Self-certification. The supplier attests to the quality of the products.

Product certification. This type of verification is based on product inspection at the customer's loading dock, extensive evaluation of the first product off a production run, third-party product evaluation, or something similar.

Quality system registration. Based on the conventional business wisdom of the 1980s, it works on the premise that one is responsible for one's own quality. Suppliers are responsible for maintaining and assuring their quality. No longer should quality be inspected. Suppliers are therefore required to have docu-

---

[1] K. Ferguson, "International Quality Standards May Affect Industry's Efforts in Europe," *Pulp and Paper*, November 1991.

mented quality systems in place and working properly. The quality audit is one mechanism of verifying this.

If the quality processes and systems are periodically audited to ensure they are satisfying internal and external customers, then this is the basis of quality assurance. If quality systems have been implemented throughout the organization and the supplier base, then this is the premise of Total Quality Management. If these systems are continuously improving, the organization's effectiveness and efficiency should be enhanced.

TYPES OF ASSESSMENT OR VERIFICATION

Depending on the product and the customer's requirements, there are three major forms of certification or verification:

First-party. This means that the supplier conducts a self-audit against the appropriate ISO 9000 standard and issues a compliance or conformance certification.

Second-party. This is common in the U.S. where the customer audits the supplier. There is much duplication as most companies have similar requirements of suppliers.

Third-party. A "certified," "qualified," or "notified" agency audits the supplier. Upon approval, the third party places the supplier on a register.[2]

Several drivers converged simultaneously to push for third-party assessments specifically for compliance to the ISO 9000 series quality standards. Drivers included:

- internationalization of business

- increased importance of standards, quality, and competitiveness

- recognition of the need for harmonization of standards and certification procedures

- increase in the amount of business being sourced to suppliers

[2] B. Rothery, *ISO 9000* (UK: Gower Publishing Co., 1991), p. 101.

- importance of suppliers as partners

- increase in supplier certification initiatives

- redundant supplier auditing

THIRD-PARTY VERIFICATION

The importance of third-party independent verification can be appreciated as more and more work in the 1990s is outsourced to often a single "world-class" supplier. A product with thousands of parts, most of which are produced by domestic if not offshore suppliers, must be specified, controlled, and assured. And as many industrial customers have discovered, problems increase in direct relation to the distance to suppliers. Suppliers will be chosen primarily on their ability to consistently produce and deliver low-cost, high-quality products and services.

In the near future, third-party verification, such as a quality systems audit, will anchor most if not all customer-supplier relationships. *The general objective of the audit is to provide "objective evidence concerning the need for the reduction, elimination, and, especially, prevention of nonconformities."*[3] An initial requirement of supplier selection may well be an audit certifying to ISO 9000. Once this hurdle is achieved, then more stringent requirements may well be placed on suppliers.

HISTORICAL BACKGROUND

ISO 9000 is not a revolutionary international quality standard. It is *evolutionary*. It evolved from existing and widely used quality standards. ISO 9000 can be traced directly to the initial military quality standard developed in 1963, MIL-Q 9858A. It evolved as well from the NATO quality standard, AQAP 1, and the British quality standard, BS 5750.

Almost all quality systems standards in the world can be traced to these roots. MIL-Q also became the template of many commercial standards, especially in regulated industries such as safety, health, aerospace, and nuclear. It was used to evaluate internal as well as a supplier's quality systems. An important part of the MIL-Q evaluation was periodic quality auditing.

[3] ISO/TC 176, "Guidelines for Auditing Quality Systems," Part 1, ISO 10011-1, 1990, p. iv.

Major ISO 9000 Milestones
1990   Food and Drug Administration (FDA) intends to replace its Good Manufacturing Practices (GMP) by ISO 9001 and additional requirements. By 1993, implementation has been uneven.
1991   Japan's Ministry of Industry and Trade (MITI) intends to adopt ISO 9000. Implementation is slow but steady. EC, Pacific Rim, and North American regulatory authorities intend to harmonize certification and tests for new pharmaceutical products.
1992   American National Standards Institute (ANSI) and Registrar Accreditation Board (RAB) form an alliance to jointly accredit registrars. National Institute for Standards and Technology (NIST) proposes the Conformity Assessment Systems Evaluation (CASE) program.

ISO Involvement in Quality

By the late 1970s, several European countries had developed quality standards that followed the NATO AQAP 1 model. In 1979 British Standards Institute (BSi) published BS 5750. Anticipating the importance of a shrinking global marketplace, the need for across-border transparency, and harmonized global quality standards, ISO formed a technical committee, TC 176, to develop an international series of quality standards.

The committee gathered representatives from various ISO-member nations to identify and develop quality criteria that would be acceptable and usable by all countries. The task was not to develop a national quality prize like the Malcolm Baldrige National Quality Award, which signifies world-class quality by high-scoring companies; the goal was to develop a sufficiently high hurdle—some call it a *minimum threshold*—that most companies could exceed. It was almost a highest common denominator of existing quality standards and one that would provide customers assurance of product quality.[4]

The American Society for Quality Control (ASQC) administers the U.S. Technical Advisory Group (TAG) to TC 176. ASQC publishes a set of technically equivalent ISO 9000 quality standards under the designation Q90 to Q94. The

[4] B. Rothery, *ISO 9000* (UK: Gower Publishing Co., 1992), pp. 8–9.

major difference between the ISO 9000 and Q90 is the substitution for British English by American word equivalents; structurally, they are the same.

The dual designations are problematic, resulting in confusion among laypeople who must understand, use, and comply with the standards. In Europe, this also has caused problems because each EC-member nation has its own designation (see the sidebar below).

ISO 9001, ISO 9002, ISO 9003, and ISO 9004 Designations

International	ISO 9001	ISO 9002	ISO 9003	ISO 9004
European	EN 29001	EN 29002	EN 29003	EN 29004
United States	ANSI/ASQC Q91	ANSI/ASQC Q92	ANSI/ASQC Q93	ANSI/ASQC Q94
The Netherlands	NEN 2646	NEN 2647	NEN 2648	NEN 2650
United Kingdom	BS 5750 Part 1	BS 5750 Part 2	BS 5750 Part 3	BS 5750 Part 0, Sec. 0.2

ISO 9000 Development

The ISO process of developing standards also follows the consensus principle. Committee Drafts (*CDs* in ISO parlance) become Draft International Standards (*DISs*) and finally an ISO Standard. The process is laborious: discussions involve word, sentence, paragraph, section, and document structuring. The level of detail and nuance discussion can leave an observer numb. However, the process works. Before a standard is fully approved, it goes through many iterations. Draft International Standards adopted by the technical committees are circulated to the ISO members. If at least 75 percent of the ISO members approve, it becomes an International Standard. Inevitably, most if not all ninety-one national signatories to ISO will bring their national quality standards into line and harmonize with ISO 9000. A similar process is now occurring among the different U.S. regulatory authorities as they align their quality standards with ISO.

International TC 176 Perspective

Dr. Horacio Martirena, an independent Argentine ISO consultant and a TC 176 member, offers the following perspective on the preparation of ISO 9000 documents:

Users of international standards (ISO 9000 series) seem to take for granted that these standards are clear, errorless documents, where every point, comma, paragraph, article, verb tense, et cetera, have been thoroughly thought out and analyzed. Experience from eight years in the Argentine Standards Institute and two years on TC 176 showed me that this is far from being the actual status of the 9000 series.

TC 176 is a group of 100–150 experts from all over the world who try to reach an agreement in two to three days every year on the draft text of the ISO 9000 standards being revised. As a member of the WG11 (working group), which deals specifically with 9001/9002/9003, I sometimes have serious doubts on our chances to issue clear and precise documents. The wording of each quality systems requirement is thoroughly discussed. However, the final wording of the standard does not always reflect the opinion or the conflicts that came out during the discussions.

My view is that as "global" standards, the 9000 series needs quite a lot of "interpretation" by the user and/or assessor. We should not consider them as the ultimate "truth," but just as basic concepts that have to be tailored for each situation in which they are applied.

Source: Personal communication

ISO 9000 Standards

Existing Standards

ISO 9000 Quality Management and Quality Assurance Standards—Guidelines for Selection and Use

ISO 9001 Quality Systems—Model for Quality Assurance in Design/ Development, Production, Installation, and Servicing

ISO 9002 Quality Systems—Model for Quality Assurance in Production and Installation

(continued on the following page)

ISO 9000 Standards (*continued*)

ISO 9003	Quality Systems—Model for Quality Assurance in Final Inspection and Test
ISO 9004	Quality Management and Quality System Elements—Guidelines
ISO 8402	Quality Management and Quality Assurance—Vocabulary

New Standards

ISO 9004-2	Quality Management and Quality System Elements—Part 2: Guidelines for Services
ISO 9000-3	Quality Management and Quality Assurance Standards—Part 3: Guidelines for the Application of ISO 9001 to the Development, Supply, and Maintenance of Software
ISO 10011-1	Guidelines for Auditing Quality Systems—Part 1: Auditing
ISO 10011-2	Guidelines for Auditing Quality Systems—Part 2: Qualification Criteria for Quality System Auditors
ISO 10011-3	Guidelines for Auditing Quality Systems—Part 3: Managing Audit Programs

Works in Progress

ISO 9000-1	Revision to ISO 9000
ISO 9000-2	Quality Management and Quality Systems Elements—Part 2: Guidelines for Implementing ISO 9001, ISO 9002, and ISO 9003
ISO 9000-4	Quality Management and Quality Assurance Standards—Part 4: Application for Dependability Management
ISO 9004-1	Revision of ISO 9004
ISO 9004-2	Quality Management and Quality Systems Elements—Part 2: Guidelines for Services
ISO 9004-3	Quality Management and Quality Systems Elements—Part 3: Guidelines for Processed Materials
ISO 9004-4	Quality Management and Quality Systems Elements—Part 4: Guidelines for Quality Improvement

ISO 9000 Standards (*continued*)
ISO 9004-5   Quality Management and Quality Systems Elements—Part 5: Guidelines for Quality Plans
ISO 9004-6   Quality Management and Quality Systems Elements—Part 6: Guidelines for Configuration Management
ISO 10012-1   Quality Assurance Requirements for Measuring Equipment— Part 1: Metrological Confirmation System for Measuring Equipment
ISO 10012-2   Quality Assurance Requirements for Measuring Equipment— Part 2: Measurement Assurance
Unnumbered   Guideline Document on Project Management
Note: Numbering for works in progress can change.

ANATOMY OF ISO 9000

The system is the solution.
—AT&T advertisement

With the intense interest on ISO 9000 there is an assumption that it is a three-hundred-page unwieldy quality document consisting of technical minutiae. This is far from the truth. As can be seen in the sidebar of systems requirements on page 77, the standards consist of twenty elements. ISO 9001, which is the most comprehensive quality standard, incorporates all twenty quality systems requirements. And the standard is only seven pages long! However, these pages are crammed-full of generic sentences that can impact a company's operations. For example, one of the twenty elements of ISO 9001 is Contract Review, and 9001 specifies that "the supplier shall establish and maintain procedures for contract review and the coordination of these activities."[5] How this is accomplished is essentially up to the supplier. The only other performance requirements spelled out in the standard are that for each contract the supplier shall (1) ensure that customer requirements are properly defined; (2) discrepancies between the customer and the supplier are resolved; (3) supplier is capable of satisfying

[5] ANSI/ASQC Q91, 1987, "Quality Systems—Model for Quality Assurance in Design/ Development, Production, Installation, and Servicing" (Geneva, Switzerland: ISO), p. 2.

contractual requirements; and (4) proper records are maintained. This is very loose in terms of evaluating and reviewing a contract. Again, how the supplier complies is a subjective decision. How the auditor evaluates the supplier's compliance should be based on the supplier's interpretation of the document, not the auditor's interpretation of how it should be done.

UNDERSTANDING ISO 9000

ISO 9000 certification rests on conforming or complying with the particular ISO 9001/9002/9003 series requirements. Two major levels of requirements are given in an organizational quality document, which is usually the quality manual. These requirements contain the organizational policies and procedures. There is a third level of detailed documents, consisting of operational documents called *workmanship standards*, which apply to and are located in a work area. The quality auditor checks these to ensure that policies and procedures are being followed.

Poor co-ordination and communication between the customer and supplier are major hindrances for developing quality products and services. ISO 9001/9002/9003 facilitate customer-supplier communication, co-ordination, and cooperation. ISO 9000 quality systems deal with almost all elements of running a company. The quality systems documents provide "shall" instructions to external suppliers in ISO 9001, ISO 9002, and ISO 9003, and indicate "should" instructions for internal quality assessments in ISO 9004.

ISO 9001, ISO 9002, or ISO 9003 registration in general indicates approval by an official body that the quality management, assurance, and control systems are in place and working properly to ensure the products and services comply with the buyer's—the customer's—requirements. The ISO 9000 standards focus on documentation, in particular the quality manual, to ensure quality systems are in place.

The ISO 9000 series is written generically, so it can be applied to a wide number of industries. As a result, each standard is open to interpretation. It becomes important to have highly trained quality auditors who understand quality systems and have specific industry experience. As well, since the series stresses quality documentation, this becomes the foundation for a total-quality, continuous-improvement effort.

A major difference between ISO 9000 series and other quality standards is its breadth. ISO 9001 specifically encompasses the entire product-development cycle, from design to disposal.

The International Organization for Standardization retains copyright of the standards, and they can be obtained from ANSI or ASQC. However, you can obtain the flavor of the standards by reviewing the Sample Quality Manual in the appendix. The quality manual is critical because it details the organizational policy and procedural issues of the twenty quality systems elements in ISO 9001.

ISO 9003, ISO 9002, ISO 9001 Systems Requirements		
ISO 9003 *12 System* *Requirements*	*ISO 9002* *18 System* *Requirements*	*ISO 9001* *20 System* *Requirements*
Management Responsibility — — → — — — — — — — — — — →		
Quality System — — — — — — → — — — — — — — — — →		
Product Identification and Traceability — — — — — — — → — — — — — — — — — →		
Inspection Status — — — — — — → — — — — — — — — — →		
Inspection and Testing — — — — → — — — — — — — — — →		
Inspection, Measuring, and Test Equipment — — — — — → — — — — — — — — — →		
Control of Nonconforming Product — — — — — — — → — — — — — — — — — →		
Handling, Storage, Packaging, and Delivery — — — — — — → — — — — — — — — — →		
Document Control — — — — — → — — — — — — — — — →		
Quality Records — — — — — — → — — — — — — — — →		
Training — — — — — — — → — — — — — — — — →		
Statistical Techniques — — — — → — — — — — — — — — →		
	Internal Auditing — — — — — — →	
	Contract Review — — — — — — →	
	Purchasing — — — — — — — →	
	Process Control — — — — — — — →	
	Purchaser Supplied Product — — — — →	
	Corrective Action — — — — — — →	
		Design Control Servicing

In some ways, the quality manual goes beyond the ISO 9001 requirements. Its value lies in the fact that it allows you to understand the generic requirements of ISO 9001.

HOW THE REGISTRATION PROCESS STARTS

The journey is the reward.
—STEVE JOBS

Registration may be imposed by a customer or may be voluntary. In the former, the customer requires a supplier to institute a quality program based on ISO 9001, ISO 9002, or ISO 9003. Or, the company, often a supplier, quickly recognizes that many customers in its particular industry sector will require similar compliance. Each time, the customer audits the supplier to evaluate compliance. This is costly to the customer and to the supplier.

Is there a way to eliminate this duplication of effort? Yes. The supplier applies to a registrar to be audited to determine compliance with the appropriate ISO 9000 series standard. Upon conforming to the standard, the registrar issues a certificate and lists the company in a directory of registered companies. The directory is accessible to all the company's customers.

CONDITION OF PARTNERING

ISO 9001/9002/9003 registration is more frequently required of suppliers that partner or have integrated operations with key customers. The reasons are many. The supplier may be given a performance specification and be asked to design a product that meets these broad requirements. In addition to these "black box" requirements, the customer may ask the supplier to design and produce the entire system, including software. For example, the supplier may have supplied just a mechanical door assembly but now is asked to supply the entire door, including electronics and glass.

Instead of inspecting all products arriving at the customer's facility, the customer may insist on ISO registration and may evaluate some prototype parts to ensure they satisfy requirements. Other than this, *ISO registration is the major assurance mechanism for assessing conformance to the customer's requirements.*

PROCEDURALIZING OPERATIONS

Almost all quality improvement comes via simplification of design, manufacturing, layout, processes, and procedures.
—TOM PETERS

ISO 9001 ensures design/development, production, installation, and servicing are fully documented and controlled. Quality documentation defines how these are controlled and ensures final customer requirements are distilled into operational criteria that are consistently followed.

Another way to view the proceduralizing of operations is in terms of quality control. The objective in quality control is to control variation around operational targets to ensure that operations are consistent and uniform with no unexpected changes to disrupt operations. Consistent operations are the major determinant of quality and satisfied customers. Most major process variables are documented, monitored, and controlled. This means that:

- the physical environment in which humidity, contaminants, or temperature remains constant;
- raw material has consistent physical and chemical properties;
- operating methods and procedures remain constant among departments, shifts, machines, and areas;
- machines, designs, fixtures, and equipment are uniform; and
- different operators run equipment similarly.

Unwanted variation can deteriorate quality by creating inconsistent operations. Variation around operational targets is defined in terms of quality standards that reflect customer requirements. These standards are operationalized into procedures and work instructions. The registrar's quality auditor verifies that procedures properly describe the work being performed. If the quality documentation exists then the auditor will interview people or observe operations to verify that the documentation reflects actual work processes.

ISO 9000—A BETTER WAY TO MANAGE

There is no universally accepted definition of Total Quality Management. The different definitions include common elements, such as customer satisfaction, worker empowerment, continuous improvement, and so on. However, it sometimes seems the concept is a catch-all for every new management concept and method. TQM is sometimes defined in terms of principles advocated by W. Edwards Deming, Joseph Juran, and Phil Crosby. Or TQM is defined using the Malcolm Baldrige criteria. The multiplicity of definitions causes confusion. *And with the push toward globalism, there is a need for a quality definition and structure that can travel across borders and be universally accepted. Why not use ISO 9000?*

Sometime in the mid-1990s, ISO 9000 quality standards will be accepted by most of the industrialized economies and may well become the globally accepted, unified platform for TQM.

International acceptance is already occurring with ISO 9001, ISO 9002, and ISO 9003. These low-level quality initiatives are becoming the vehicle for a uniform concept of quality. The problem is that they are easily attainable quality floors.

But what about quality ceilings, stretch benchmarks for companies? What's available to urge companies to higher levels of achievement and continuous improvement? There is the Malcolm Baldrige National Quality Award, and the European Quality Award.

ISO 9004 and other ISO guidelines may well define TQM in the 1990s. ISO 9004 is a series of quality system guidelines. While ISO 9001, ISO 9002, and ISO 9003 are "shall" documents, ISO 9004 is a series of "should" documents or guides listing suggested advanced quality practices in different areas, functions, and product sectors. These are ideal for conducting internal audits.

These guideline documents are expanding to incorporate such components as processed materials, software, and services. Why aren't these incorporated into ISO 9001, ISO 9002, or ISO 9003? These quality standards are contractual. Once a company has been registered to these standards, adding more requirements would require a reaudit each time there is a new quality document. The committee responsible for writing ISO 9000 decided to incorporate improvements and changes into the guideline documents and periodically, every five years or so, change the requirement—"shall"—documents.

It's interesting to note that some companies are adopting ISO 9004 and changing the "shoulds" to "shalls." The "shalls" are then incorporated into the contract or purchase order.

Let's look at some of the other ISO 9000 documents:

Service Industries

ISO 9000 series of quality standards is an evolving document. It was originally intended to focus on product quality. The problem is obvious. A product may include intangible service elements that are as important as the tangible product elements. For example, a restaurant meal is a mixture of food, service, and ambience.

ISO 9004-2, "Guidelines for Services," was developed "to provide a systematic approach to quality management aimed at ensuring that customer needs are understood and met." The standard goes on: "The achievement of quality necessitates a commitment to quality principles at all levels in the organization and a continual review and improvement of the established system of quality management based on feedback of the customer's perceptions of the service provided."[6]

Quality Plans

ISO 9004-5, "Guidelines for Quality Plans," provides direction for how to develop quality assurance plans for hardware, software, processed material, and services. The purpose of the quality assurance plan is to define the quality work activities and how they will be carried out in a contract, project, or product. A quality plan may include quality objectives, accountabilities, procedures/work instructions, types of testing, locations of activities, documentation, and changes in activity. Again, the purpose is to have the supplier know what needs to be done to satisfy the customer and do it according to logical plan. A quality plan is not currently part of ISO 9001, ISO 9002, or ISO 9003 quality systems elements; however, it will be in future revisions of these standards.

A Caveat

There is a danger that ISO series of quality documents may become the basis of running an organization. While conducting an audit, the quality auditor may state or imply that these documents ensure competitiveness. The auditee, the company being audited, thinks this is how a company should be run. The company president buys the ISO 9000 guidelines and changes the way the organization is managed.

ISO 9000 guidelines were not developed nor intended to be mandates, just broad guidelines for developing quality systems, not operational decision criteria. The ISO documents should not supplant good business sense and clear decision making.

---

[6] "Quality Management and Quality System Elements—Part 2: Guidelines for Services" (Geneva, Switzerland: ISO, 1991), p. iii.

ISO 9000 AUDITING EXPERIENCES

Third-party auditing is the method of ensuring compliance to either ISO 9001, ISO 9002, or ISO 9003. The auditors are employed by registrars whose function is to maintain the list of qualified suppliers. Many U.S. quality auditors took lead assessor training to conduct ISO systems audits from the British Institute for Quality Auditors (IQA) approved material. Until 1992, there was no U.S. nationally approved quality auditor training course. The Registrar Accreditation Board (RAB), part of the American Society for Quality Control, has developed a certified course for lead quality auditors. (This topic is covered in detail in Chapter 7.)

The British were early adopters of the standard and probably have more experience than anyone conducting ISO 9000 or BS 5750 quality audits. There are more than twenty thousand registered companies in the UK, far more than in any other country. The application of the standard is very broad. Manufacturing firms, service businesses, municipalities, schools, and organizations in almost every industry have been quality audited in the UK. The breadth of the organizations using ISO 9000 reflects well on its applicability.

QUALITY AUDITING PROCEDURE

ISO 9000 and BS 5750 registration indicates that an organization has quality systems in place in different areas of the organization. Quality auditors, or as they are sometimes called *quality assessors*, follow a commonly accepted process.

First, the auditors conduct a preliminary assessment. It involves reviewing the auditee's quality documentation, which includes the quality manual and other supporting materials. This evaluation determines if the auditee's quality documentation satisfies the certification level being sought. If the auditor believes that something is missing or an ISO 9000 element is not addressed, the auditor informs the auditee and waits until the item has been addressed before conducting the on-site visit.

Next, the auditor visits the auditee, the company, to determine the level of compliance between "what is" and "what should be" as specified by ISO 9001/9002/9003. This usually means the auditor will visit a specific area to ensure that procedures are followed. The auditor may interview people, investigate corrective actions, analyze flowcharts, or conduct other analyses.

Registration is usually by discrete site or process. If there are multiplant or site operations, each must be audited separately, and each is awarded its own registration certificate. At this stage, costs can multiply quickly if each site is audited. The other option is to secure a multi-site certificate. The auditor then statistically samples and assesses quality systems in selected plants.

The auditor often will work off a tailored checklist of questions that address the particular ISO 9000 criteria. For example, three questions under the "Management Responsibility" system may be:

- Do contract requirements spell out product performance and/or product quality attributes?

- Do the supplier's documents define quality policies, objectives, and procedures?

- Does the supplier's organization understand the importance of quality?

There are three choices of responses beside each question: Yes, No, or N/A (Not Applicable). Anytime there is a No response, the auditor issues a Corrective Action Request (CAR). The purpose of the CAR is to eliminate the symptom and the root cause of the problem. If no discrepancies are subsequently found and if corrective action has been implemented, then registration to the specified level is recommended. Following registration, regular and announced six-month surveillance visits ensure that quality systems and standards are maintained.[7] Most ISO 9000 quality auditing follows this procedure. (The auditing cycle is described in more detail in Chapter 7.)

FUTURE ISO 9000 STANDARDS DEVELOPMENT

ISO 9000 standards are written generically by a number of national representatives. They can be applied to almost any industry—a "one size fits all" approach. A problem could arise because the standards are written broadly; that is, the company seeking registration will interpret them narrowly for its specific system, process, or product application, and the auditor subsequently will ensure compliance to the broadly written standard. As well, the document numbering system is confusing. It seems that every country uses essentially the same document but numbers it differently. This may be simply national hubris. New works in progress

---

[7] J. Heap, "Quality and BS 5750," *Management Services*, March 1991, pp. 22–23.

are continuously being developed. Whatever the reason, there are multiple designations for the same standard, as indicated by the sidebar on page 72, "ISO 9001, ISO 9002, ISO 9003, and ISO 9004 Designations."

VISION 2000

Where are ISO 9000 series of quality standards going? Quality systems certification is becoming a global trade issue. ISO TC 176 intended to standardize the development of the standard, its numbering system, and its implementation. This effort and the subsequent report were called Vision 2000.

Four strategic goals for ISO 9000 and related standards were proposed in Vision 2000:

Universal acceptance. The series of standards have wide application in different industries or product categories. As well, the standards satisfy customer requirements and are user-friendly.

Current compatibility. Document numbering is compatible and supports existing ISO documents.

Forward compatibility. Revisions of the standards are minor and evolutionary. Revisions don't constrain implementation, especially in enforceable clauses or standards.

Forward flexibility. Supplements to the standards are few and, if developed, are broadly applicable.

Since ISO 9001/9002/9003 are contractual standards, changes must be evolutionary. Understandable, usable, and flexible are the ISO code words and a strong market focus is essential. If the standards are industry specific, difficult to use, require a quantum stretch, or offer other constraints, they simply won't be used. The standards require voluntary adoption. TC 176 cannot legislate or mandate international, national, industry, or company adoption.[8]

To understand the accelerating importance of ISO 9000, EC standards development must be understood, and is covered in the next chapter.

---

[8] D. Marquardt, J. Chove, K. Jensen, J. Pyle, D. Strahle, "Vision 2000: The Strategy for ISO Series Standards in the 1990s," *Quality Progress*, May 1991, pp. 25–31.

CHAPTER 5

EC Conformity Assessment

Interdependence recreates the world in the image of a global village.
—MARSHALL McLUHAN, Futurist

ISO 9000 third-party audits are but one element of a larger set of conformity assessment issues. Conformity assessment is the process for providing the assurance that each country's products conform to standards, specifications, contracts, or codes. The eventual goal will be to have products throughout the world conform to technical standards and pass conformity tests.

"NEW APPROACH" DIRECTIVES

How can you govern a country with two hundred and forty-six varieties of cheese?

—CHARLES DE GAULLE

The development of EC standards and the mechanisms to ensure conformance was initiated in the 1980s. In 1985 the EC adopted the "New Approach" to standards making, which were spelled out in the White Paper, "Completing the

Internal Market." Under this approach, the EC Commission issued directives for vertical groups of products that dealt with health, safety, and the environment.

The directive is the EC's main rule-making and harmonization mechanism for implementing economic integration. More than half of the 279 initial directives dealt with product standards. Directives may define product-safety requirements, conformity assessment methods, and application dates.

Before 1985 the EC had attempted to harmonize technical standards by creating very detailed product specifications. The level of detail was considered anticompetitive in terms of constraining innovation and risk taking. The "New Approach" to standards development was less detailed. It focused on a product's "essential requirements," which were basically its safety characteristics. These essential characteristics at first applied only to those product categories that specifically addressed safety, health and environmental issues.

Two Elements of the New Approach

The New Approach introduced two important concepts: harmonized European standards and mutual recognition.[1]

Harmonized European Standards

Under this approach, directives were developed in health, safety, consumer protection, and environmental protection areas. Directives were then developed for simple pressure vessels, natural-gas appliances, medical devices, and other products. (See the sidebar on page 88 for a complete list of regulated products.)

Technical standards relating to specific standards were then generated by the European Committee for Standardization (CEN) and the European Committee for Electrotechnical Standardization (CENELEC).[2]

Mutual Recognition

The principle of mutual recognition states that EC-member nations must allow the free movement of products without having to be modified, tested, certified,

[1] International Trade Commission, "The Effects of Greater Economic Integration Within the European Community on the U.S.: First Follow-Up Report," ISITC Pub. 2268 (Washington, D.C.: Superintendent of Documents, 1990), pp. 6–9.

[2] Scottish Development Agency brochure "1992 Issues: Product Regulatory Standardization," May 1989.

or renamed. Exceptions may be made when public safety and health issues are involved. In these product areas, some form of conformity assessment, such as registration to ISO 9001, may be authorized.

The principle of mutual recognition between national authorities was formally established and accepted following the Cassis de Dijon Decision. *The Court decided that a legally developed product in one member state must be accepted and admitted by other member states.* The mutual recognition principle was integrated into the White Paper, "Completing the Internal Market," which set the agenda for EC integration. This principle also became an important element of the global harmonization of technical standards.

The White Paper advocated the removal of physical, technical, and fiscal barriers that deter the establishment of a single, unified economic market. For example, if a company wanted to manufacture medical devices, the manufacturer's home country would be responsible for regulating and authorizing their design, production, and distribution. If the company met the essential national safety requirements, it would be free to design, manufacture, and distribute through the EC without being licensed or supervised by the other EC countries, which would recognize the home country's authority, competence, and monitoring abilities. Why not expand this principle to make the technical barriers transparent around the world?

This concept became the foundation for the global acceptance of products based on mutually recognized testing and certification. The Europeans intended to establish Mutual Recognition Agreements (MRAs) for the testing of regulated products and the certification of quality systems with countries outside the EC. The thrust behind these agreements is that the country will serve as "guarantor" for its national testing and certification agencies that approve regulated products.

REGULATED PRODUCTS

High profits stem largely from superior execution or forceful opportunism, not structural competitive barriers.
—AMER BHIDE, Educator

An important distinction can now be made: the difference between regulated and unregulated products. *Regulated products are those covered by EC directives. Unregulated are those not specifically addressed by an EC directive.*

Cassis de Dijon Decision

A German firm, Rewe, attempted to import a French liqueur, crème de cassis, into West Germany. German law forbade the importation of liqueurs containing alcohol below a specified level. The French firm appealed to the European Court of Justice, which ruled that the Germans could not block a product that was already sold in France, except for health, fair trade, consumer protection, or fiscal reasons. The Court established that the burden of proof was with the importing country to prove that products legally produced and marketed in the EC did not comply with safety, health, consumer protection, or environmental regulations.

Two legal principles dealing with the harmonization of technical standards were thus established:

1. A product or group of products that met essential safety criteria must be allowed free circulation within Europe.

2. If there are differences among products that are based on nonessential requirements, there must be "mutual recognition" of national regulations and industrial standards.*

*R. Williams, M. Teagan, and J. Beneyto, *The World's Largest Market* (New York: AMACOM), pp. 5–6.

EC New Approach Directives

In order to develop a single internal market for products and services, the EC is harmonizing hundreds of national policies, regulations, laws, and specifications dealing with many industrial products.

The list of some of the adopted, proposed, and planned directives as well as their implementation dates and transition periods are listed below. Integration is occurring much slower than Brussels technocrats anticipated, so these dates may be moved forward.

Adopted	*Implementation Date*	*Transition Period*
Toys	1/1/90	None
Simple Pressure Vessels	7/1/90	7/1/92

EC New Approach Directives (*continued*)

Adopted	Implementation Date	Transition Period
Construction Products	6/27/91	Indefinite
Electromagnetic Compatibility	1/1/92	12/31/95
Natural-Gas Appliances	1/1/92	12/31/95
Personal Protective Equipment	7/1/92	None
Machinery	12/31/92	12/31/94*
Nonautomatic Weighing Instruments	1/1/93	1/1/2003
Active Implantable Medical Devices	1/1/93	12/31/94
Type Approval of Telecommunications Terminal Equipment	11/6/92	None
Proposed		
Medical Devices	7/1/94	6/30/97
Elevators	—	—
Equipment for Use in Explosives Atmospheres	—	—
Planned		
In-Vitro Diagnostics	—	—
Flammability of Furniture	—	—
Pressure Equipment	—	—
Measuring and Testing Instruments	—	—
Recreational Craft	—	—
Cable Ways	—	—
Amusement Park and Fairground Equipment	—	—
Playground Equipment (includes sports equipment)	—	—
Used Machinery	—	—
Fasteners	—	—

* Additional restrictions

Source: International Trade Administration, "EC Product Standards Under the Internal Market Program" (Washington, D.C.: Superintendent of Documents), April 1, 1992.

Harmonization first focused on regulated products and then is being extended to include unregulated products. *It's estimated that 50 percent or $50 billion of U.S. exports to the EC are subject to its harmonization requirements.*[3]

This is where the previously discussed mutual recognition principle comes into play. If a product is unregulated, then the EC will recognize national standards covering nonsafety-related product characteristics. The mutual recognition principle is being elevated to a global trade-policy issue among countries.

What does this mean to an exporter to Europe that hasn't conformed to the international equivalent standard? If an unregulated product conforms to a U.S. national standard and if an EC-member country accepts the U.S. national standard as equivalent to theirs, then the product can be marketed in the EC.

Some of the EC directives that specify essential requirements in regulated products are construction products, telecommunications terminal devices, electromagnetic compatibility, and natural-gas appliance directives. These are briefly discussed below. The compliance or conformance mechanisms called modules are described later in the chapter.

CONSTRUCTION PRODUCTS DIRECTIVE

On December 21, 1988, the EC issued the Construction Products Directive, which defined construction products as those "produced for incorporation in a permanent manner in construction works, including both building and civil engineering works." The essential requirements in this directive cover six general areas: mechanical resistance and stability; safety in case of fire; hygiene, health, and the environment; safety in use; protection against noise; energy economy and heat retention.[4]

TELECOMMUNICATIONS TERMINAL EQUIPMENT DIRECTIVE

The Terminal Equipment Directive covers seven essential requirements, including user safety, protection of the network from harm, and interworking with network equipment.[5]

---

[3] International Trade Administration, "EC Product Standards Under the Internal Market Program" (Washington, D.C.: Superintendent of Documents), April 1, 1992, p. 1.

[4] D. Mackay, "EC 1992 and the Construction Products Directive," ASTM Standardization News, February 1992, p. 48.

[5] M. Saunders, "EC-Wide Certification of Telecom Terminal Equipment Scheduled to Start in November," *Europe Now: A Report*, Washington, D.C.: U.S. Department of Commerce, July–August 1992, p. 4.

ELECTROMAGNETIC COMPATIBILITY (EMC) DIRECTIVE

This directive covers all equipment that is capable of causing an electromagnetic disturbance or of being affected by one. The list of potential products is huge. It includes radios, TVs, appliances, mobile radios, information technology devices, telecommunications equipment, industrial manufacturing equipment, and scientific equipment. The directive generally states that radiation generated by the above products cannot interfere with radio and telephone operations.[6]

NATURAL-GAS APPLIANCE DIRECTIVE

The directive mandates safety levels of natural-gas appliances and safety devices by specifying design, operating characteristics, and inspection procedures. The purpose of the directive is similar to the others in that it ensures safety criteria are harmonized from one EC member state to another.

The essential requirements of the gas directive dictate that products:

- are designed and constructed to operate safely;
- have the appropriate technical instructions, service information, and warning notices; and
- are constructed of materials that can withstand the applicable technical, chemical, and thermal conditions.

As the stuff of competitiveness, the directives are dull and difficult to wade through. The following essential requirement from the gas directive is typical of the dense prose in the directives: "All pressurized parts of an appliance must withstand the mechanical and thermal stress to which they are subjected without any deformation affecting safety."[7]

TRANSITION BLUES

The EC is falling behind in implementing its harmonization scheme for a single market because the European standards-making bodies (CEN/CENELEC/

[6] B. G. Simson, "Conformity Assessment Workshop on Electromagnetic Compatibility," Washington, D.C.: U.S. Department of Commerce, 1991, p. 4.

[7] Council Directive, "Approximation of the Laws of the Member States," June 29, 1990, p. L196/21.

ETSI) with whom it contracted to write the technical standards have been slow in developing them.

With the growing backlog, the directives have been amended to include a transition period of two to four years to allow time for standards to be developed and sufficient time for testing facilities to be qualified and authorized. During this time, manufacturers can continue to produce to existing national requirements and standards rather than complying with new EC requirements.[8]

The Toy Directive was the first directive to be implemented. This seemed fairly safe to pilot. But problems immediately erupted. Originally, only six EC-member nations wanted to implement the directive. One option was to allow manufacturers to self-certify products. However, some member countries were not willing to accept self-certification as a means to demonstrate conformity. If this problem occurred with a relatively simple directive, what would happen when directives became more complex and the economic stakes with each directive became higher?

ONE PRODUCT—MULTIPLE DIRECTIVES

EC directives set floors, or in other words, minimum legal health and safety requirements, for products from toys to medical devices to natural-gas appliances. It's important for a manufacturer to understand the specifics of a directive. For example, an information technology equipment manufacturer may have to comply with a minimum of four specific directives, the EMC Directive, the Low-Voltage Directive on Electrical Safety, the Telecommunications Terminal Equipment Directive, and the Ergonomics Directive for Visual Display Terminals.[9]

Or, a commercial air-conditioning manufacturer may have to comply with three separate directives, specifically Machine Safety, Pressure Vessels, and Construction Products.[10]

[8] International Trade Administration, "EC Testing and Certification Procedures Under the Internal Market Program," April 1, 1992, p. 9.

[9] B. G. Simson, "Conformity Assessment Workshop on Electromagnetic Compatibility," Washington, D.C.: U.S. Department of Commerce, 1991, p. 4.

[10] B. G. Simson, "Conformity Assessment on Pressure Vessels," Washington, D.C.: U.S. Department of Commerce, 1991, p. 42.

LACK OF U.S. INPUT

At first, EC standards development was disregarded in the U.S. Recently, U.S. companies concerned with a slowing domestic economy realized that foreign markets represented opportunities for growth. The problem was that the Europeans in many instances were ignoring U.S. standards and developing their own. Much of the industrialized world feared that the Europeans would develop technical standards that would restrict the entry of their products.

Non-EC and non-EFTA countries are not partners in the CEN/CENELEC standards-making groups. The U.S. and other countries have requested observer status in order to track and provide input to the standards development process. And, the number of standards are continually increasing in complexity. *The issue for many U.S. companies, and more critically for small U.S. companies, is access to these standards-making discussions.*

In terms of global testing and certification, the conformity assessment mechanisms for regulated as well as nonregulated products have not been implemented in the U.S. or the rest of the world. There is still much reluctance to accept test results from another country.

GLOBAL TESTING AND CERTIFICATION

Thousands of national technical standards exist in the EC. The standards have been used to hinder the flow of products across European national boundaries. Conceivably, a company planning to market products throughout Europe would have to comply with twelve different technical standards in nine different languages with different requirements, paying fees in each country.[11] This becomes more complicated if a company wants to market products globally. Tens of thousands of standards could hinder global trade.

The critical issue is to ensure that certification and test results are compatible across borders. Compatibility would eventually lead to global transparency, the unhindered movement of products throughout the world.

---

[11] S. Harlan, "ISO 9000: The Wave of the Future" (New York: KPMG, Peat Marwick, March/April 1992), pp. 1–2.

INTERNATIONAL MUTUAL RECOGNITION AGREEMENTS

How would this be accomplished? One mechanism is for governments to negotiate nation-to-nation Mutual Recognition Agreements whereby each country certifies its own testing and certification structure, similar to what is shown in the figure on page 95.

Each level of the pyramid would certify the credibility of the certification group below it. At the top of the pyramid is a national certifying body. These groups would negotiate agreements with counterpart national groups, mostly on a regulated sector-by-sector basis. Nonregulated products would be negotiated by national industry groups. In regulated sectors, U.S. national agencies would be the focal point of the negotiations, such as the National Institute for Standards and Technology for building products, the Food and Drug Administration for medical devices, or the Consumer Product Safety Commission for toys. Each of these federal agencies already regulates products in the U.S.

The recognizing bodies would then certify accreditors primarily in regulated industry sectors. There may be similar voluntary efforts in the nonregulated sectors. Accreditors may also be private standards developing organizations. For example, the American Society of Mechanical Engineers has already been registering pressure vessels for a number of years. It therefore makes sense for ASME to formally serve accreditor or registrar functions for pressure vessels.

Accreditors then certify registrars and their quality systems auditors. The registrars conduct the ISO 9000 systems audits and maintain the register of approved supplier/companies. The registrars also conduct the six-month surveillance audits.

The entire structure is based on credibility and trust. If any one level is suspect, then the entire model of global certification becomes suspect.

How is the system presently running? It is in a state of flux. The model is taking shape slowly in both the EC and the U.S. while credibility and trust are being developed. In the regulated sectors progress will come more quickly because these products come under governmental supervision, and the regulatory structure is already in place. In the nonregulated side progress is slower. Presently, the recognition of test results is being conducted through Memoranda of Understanding or cross-certifications between one nation's registrars and another's, or between one nation's registrars and another's national accrediting bodies. And, the level of MOUs can range from "we agree to agree to talk" to "full acceptance of the other party's test results."

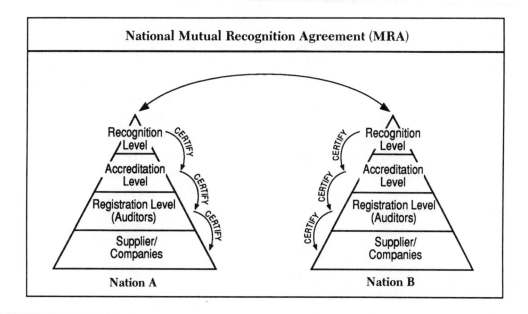

National Mutual Recognition Agreement (MRA)

CONFORMITY ASSESSMENT MODULES

According to Dr. C. A. J. Simons of Philips Electronics, global certification and testing has three requirements:

1. Consensus about assessment methods

2. Mutual recognition of test results and certificates/marks by third parties

3. Acceptance by authorities/end users/customers of the results of the conformity assessment[12]

The first issue is to form a consensus about assessment methods. The principal purpose of the conformity assessment procedures is to facilitate product transparency. The official European position is: *"The essential objective of a conformity assessment is to enable the public authorities to ensure that products placed on the market conform to the requirements as expressed in the provisions of the directives, in particular with regard to the health and safety of users and consumers."*[13]

[12] Personal communication

[13] "Conformity Assessment Procedures in the Technical Harmonization Directives," Official Journal of the European Communities, No. L 380/14–15, December 13, 1990.

Conformity assessment is divided into eight modules—A through H—which address both production and design. The conformity assessment modules offer the manufacturer a range of possible options to comply with the specific directive. The type of assessment is determined by the type of product, nature of risks, and required level of assurance. These factors are detailed in the particular EC Commission directives. Obviously, high-risk safety and health products require a higher level of assurance.[14]

The modules are a cookbook approach to certification that can be used by most industries in all countries. It should be mentioned as well that these modules are minimums or floors for determining the quality or the conformity of products. Additional requirements may be imposed.

The eight modules are:

Module A: Internal Control of Production

In self-certification, the supplier or product manufacturer provides assurance directly to the customer that the product conforms to requirements. The manufacturer affixes a certification label or mark to each product and maintains technical documentation which can be reviewed by the appropriate parties. Technical documentation consists of all relevant material that would enable the conformity of the material to be assessed. It may include a general description of the product, conceptual design and manufacturing drawings, explanations for interpreting the drawings, lists of applicable standards, design calculations, and tests conducted. This module is not being used as widely as anticipated, largely due to perceived risks and customers wanting higher levels of assurance.

Module B: Type Examination

The manufacturer sends a representative sample product from a production run and technical documentation to a government *notified* or *certified* body for testing to ensure the product meets specified requirements. The assessment of a representative product or specimen is commonly called *type examination*.

The notified body examines the sample product to ensure it has been manufactured according to the technical documentation, relevant standards, and directive essential requirements. The notified body also conducts relevant tests to

---

[14] Ibid.

ensure it conforms to all applicable requirements. Upon passing these tests, the manufacturer is issued an EC type–examination certificate. This module is often accompanied by another type of conformity assessment, such as a quality systems audit, as can be seen in the figure on page 98.

Module C: Conformity to Type

Modules C through F are used with Module B. The manufacturer, in addition to the previous tests and evaluation by a notified body, declares the products conform with the EC type–examination certificate of Module B and satisfies the requirements of the applicable EC directive. Then, the manufacturer can affix a certification mark to each product.

It should be mentioned that the above requirements are minimums and that supplemental requirements may be imposed. For example, the notified body may check and test products at random intervals during production.

Module D: Production Quality Assurance (ISO 9002)

Module D describes the procedure in which the manufacturer declares the product is in conformity with type, Module B; satisfies the applicable EC directive; operates an approved production quality system that complies with ISO 9002; and is periodically audited by a third-party registrar. The Europeans want the third-party audits conducted by government approved bodies. Third-party quality system audits are becoming the dominant form of conformity assessment.

Module E: Product Quality Assurance (ISO 9003)

In this module, the manufacturer first satisfies Module B, declares conformity, and then must comply and be certified to the twelve quality system requirements in ISO 9003.

Module F: Product Verification

In this module, a manufacturer attests that products conform to type and satisfies the applicable directive. Depending on the requirements of the specific directive, a notified body may examine and test the conformity of every product or of a

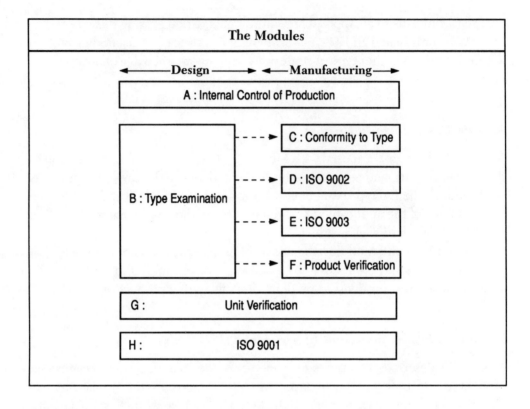

few by statistically sampling the production run. If statistical sampling is chosen, the manufacturer first determines that production runs produce homogeneous products, then random, representative samples can be selected from a production run.

Module G: Unit Verification

The manufacturer ensures and declares a single product conforms to the applicable directive and other requirements. A notified body then examines and conducts the appropriate tests on individual products to ensure conformity.

Module H: Full Quality Assurance (ISO 9001)

This is probably the most prevalent conformity assessment module. It is a full third-party quality assessment of all twenty ISO 9001 quality systems elements.

MISINFORMATION OR DISINFORMATION

"You have to be ISO 9000 registered to do business in the EC," is much-repeated. The comment is true for only some regulated products, and for these there are alternative means or modules for complying.

Why is all this "disinformation" occurring? Jim Highlands, a member of the U.S. Technical Advisory Group to TC 176, speculates:

Global standardization is actually a useful tool in that it provides an efficient method of communicating information and thereby facilitates trade among nations. However, it suffers one critical flaw: that is, when the *standards committee is done writing the document and throws it over the transom, so to speak, the marketplace is welcome to utilize the document in any manner it sees fit.* This can be seen in a proliferation of ISO 9000 consulting. The somewhat simple subject/document is made increasingly complex as the number of individuals willing to provide advice on it increases.

The problem becomes exacerbated. He continues:

Few practicing consultants know of the EC module system or its intended function for controlled (regulated) products. This is evidenced by the fact that typical advice by consultants to prospective clients is "You will not be able to do business with Europe or anyone else who does business with Europe unless you are [ISO] registered." This is not only false, but borders on being malicious gossip.[15]

CE MARK

Product certification marks on consumer and commercial products are common in the U.S. Underwriters Laboratories affixes its mark on electrical products; the American Gas Association on natural gas appliances; and the American Society of Mechanical Engineers (ASME) on pressure vessels. The CE mark is the EC certification symbol of conformity assessment to the specific requirements of a directive. The CE mark indicates compliance with EC safety, health, and consumer legal and regulatory requirements. Again, there is confusion

---

[15] Personal communication

even among the EC-member countries about how the CE mark should be used. A product may have to conform with more than one directive. The CE mark would therefore indicate conformity to all EC directives that relate to the product.

The design of the CE mark was prescribed by the Commission. Two identification numerals, as seen in the figure below, are attached to the mark. The first identifies the year in which the mark was affixed and the second identifies the notified or certification body.

$$C\,E\ 94\ 056$$

The rules for using the CE mark of conformity are:

- can be used only on industrial products

- ascertains conformity to all legal requirements

- applies only for the New Approach Directives

- is used by the manufacturer only

- must be used according to the rules, otherwise the penalty is removal of the product from the market

CE Mark Is Not Necessarily a Quality Mark

A common misinterpretation is that the CE mark signifies product safety and functional quality. It doesn't. The mark primarily indicates compliance with the product's specific legal requirements, the so-called "essential requirements" dealing with safety, health, and environmental criteria.[16]

Harry Gundlach, general manager of Raad voor de Certificate (RvC), differentiates between the functional and safety-related aspects of quality as follows:

[16] International Trade Administration, "EC Testing and Certification Procedures Under the Internal Market Program," April 1, 1992, p. 9.

There is a general feeling that the CE mark is a tool to cross borders and not a sign of product quality. Quality can be defined as "fitness of intended use." It embraces two related ideas: the product should do what it is intended to do and should not produce unwanted side-effects; it must be safe, et cetera. In some cases, the differences between these is marginal; for instance, in the case of a pacemaker. In other cases, there is a major difference; for instance, in the case of blue asbestos, which is an excellent insulator but has a fatal disadvantage of being carcinogenic."[17]

Another problem is that a user may think the CE mark indicates compliance to all regulations and requirements. But a product may have to carry additional conformity marks. For example, pressure vessels, addressed in one of the directives, must be certified by a notified body before it can be marketed in the EC, but the customer may still insist that a U.S. manufacturer satisfy American Society of Mechanical Engineers standards and carry the ASME mark.

PRODUCT LIABILITY

A major reason for pursuing ISO registration is to limit product liability exposure. The EC's strict liability law covers cases throughout the Community. The law makes the manufacturers responsible for damages, losses, and injuries caused by product defects, regardless of fault or negligence.

What are possible defenses? The Department of Commerce's International Trade Administration has opined that it would depend to which standard the manufacturer was complying and how conformance was assessed. The ITA offers the following interpretation:

> However, it is widely believed that a manufacturer who has met all the legal requirements in EC directives, has certified to any existing EC-wide standards, and has placed all the adequate warnings and labels on a product will have a stronger defense in any possible liability suit. One of the defenses to a liability claim is if the producer can show that the product complies with mandatory regulation issued by public authorities. . . . Even if voluntary standards are not mentioned as a defense

---

[17] H. Gundlach, "The Role of Accreditation and the Route to the CE Mark" (Driebergen, Netherlands: RvC, 1991), p. 7.

under the EC liability law, a manufacturer who has certified to European standards will stand on strong ground in a liability claim.[18]

In regards to the second issue of how a company indicates conformity assessment, the ITA states:

There is a debate currently going that asserts that a manufacturer may have a stronger defense in a liability suit if she/he has a quality system registered to the International Organization for Standardization 9000 series of standards. . . . Having these documents on hand and also having the mark of an accredited quality registrar who performed the registration may assist or protect the producer in the case of a liability claim.[19]

EUROPEAN ORGANIZATION FOR TESTING AND CERTIFICATION (EOTC)

The Cassis de Dijon Decision concluded that the EC-member nations could not prohibit the sale of products legally produced and marketed in one of the member countries. But how could one country ensure that all goods produced and sold in one country were compatible to those in other countries? The issue focused on the development of mechanisms for ensuring the technical equivalence or transparency of regulated as well as unregulated products. Equivalence would only be reached if there was agreement on the testing and certification procedures—the modules discussed in the previous section in both regulated and unregulated product sectors. The purpose of the EOTC was to bring pertinent parties in various industry sectors to the table to reach agreement on the testing and certification procedures.[20]

The EOTC has expressed its mission as:

EOTC has the goal of establishing mutual confidence between all parties concerned with conformity assessment issues, so as to facilitate the free circulation,

[18] International Trade Administration, "EC Product Standards Under the Internal Market Program," April 1, 1992, p. 11.

[19] Ibid., p. 12.

[20] "The Developing Role of the EOTC for the Single European Market," pp. 1–3, *Testing and Certification in Europe*: The role of the EOTC, Proceedings, 1992.

throughout Europe, of goods and services that have demonstrated conformity with technical specifications.[21]

SECTORAL COMMITTEES AND AGREEMENT GROUPS

Sectoral committees and agreement groups are two key groups in the EOTC. The purpose of the sectoral committees is to coordinate the activities of agreements groups. Sectoral committees are represented by national delegations consisting of manufacturers, users, and certifications bodies for a specific industry sector. For example, an electrotechnology sectoral group works on its conformity assessment issues. Within the sectoral committee, agreement groups composed of testing and certification bodies and other interested parties negotiate agreements that bind them to mutually recognize test and certification results. Testing laboratories and certification bodies make the agreements as private parties and as technical professionals without direct government intervention or involvement. This underscores an important point, specifically that the parties that have the most to gain, the certification bodies, are helping to direct the EOTC's actions and are voluntarily forming the agreements.[22]

MULTIPLE STAKEHOLDERS

Part of the EOTC's challenge is to balance and to represent many diverse views in such a way that no one special-interest group dominates. The EOTC represents many divergent European stakeholders, including manufacturers and consumers.

The EOTC's stakeholders are: "Suppliers, purchasers, and users of goods and services, and the conformity assessment practitioners (test laboratories, inspection bodies, certification bodies) who will benefit from the development, promotion, and use of common procedures."[23]

Nils Ringstedt, a Swedish consumer advocate on the EOTC board, expressed the consumer perspective:

[21] EOTC, "European Organization for Testing and Certification, 1991," Brussels, Belgium: EOTC Office, 1991, p. 7.

[22] "Countdown to the Mature Stage," EOTC Factsheet Number 8, May 1992.

[23] "EOTC Open for Business," EOTC Factsheet Number 5, June 1991.

Conformity assessment in the form of testing and certification must rely on standards with a high reliability and which give the same results wherever they are used. Otherwise, the consumer's confidence in assessment will be lost. Therefore, consumer influence on standardization is extremely important to create confidence for the products marketed. Active participation in standardization by consumer representatives should aim at safeguarding the consumer's interests as regards safety, function, energy, and environment.[24]

SLOW BUT STEADY PROGRESS

Eurocrats are dismayed that their economic and political union is occurring so slowly. Some Community members such as Denmark are expressing second thoughts of political union. Other members are uncomfortable with surrendering control of visible elements of sovereignty such as currency, foreign affairs, and domestic policy. And the smaller countries are afraid of ceding political, cultural, and economic control to the larger EC states such as Germany and France.[25]

However, the process of economic integration has started and won't stop. It is a slow and inconsistent march toward technical, economic, and political union. In some areas, each step is haltingly slow, and in other areas, each step seems to result in two steps backwards. The halting steps forward are found in the areas of technical harmonization of standards and testing. The steps backwards are those entailed in the Maastricht Agreement, which are in the areas of common currency, foreign policy, and intertrade policies.

What happens if the original twelve countries don't form their political union? There's consensus that at least they will form an economic union consisting of a loose trading federation of open borders and harmonized technical standards. Most pundits maintain that harmonization of standards and trade will continue because technical issues don't elicit the visceral response that culture and currency do, and most people understand the need for common technical standards when traveling twenty miles and entering a new country.

Will full integration come to pass? Probably not within the optimistic and sometimes unrealistic timelines that were initially envisioned by the Eurocrats.

[24] Personal communication

[25] C. Whitney, "Europe to Press Union Votes Despite Denmark's Rejection," *New York Times*, June 5, 1992, p. A4.

However, the process has started. Most EC members realize that they have an unparalleled opportunity to influence global economic and environmental affairs through GATT and technical standardization. Germany, France, the United Kingdom, and Italy will not let these opportunities slip by. The process is irreversible, and its impact is going to be felt globally, including in the U.S.

The basic question is Will there evolve a transparent global conformity assessment system dealing with standards, quality system testing, product certification, and testing. Yes. However, it will take much time, probably beyond the year 2000. In the next chapter, we examine the conformity assessment struggles in the U.S.

CHAPTER 6

U.S. Conformity Assessment

What do we want our kids to do? Sweep around Japanese computers?
—WALTER MONDALE, 1982

An important element of American trade policy in the 1990s is to increase exports, thereby producing high-wage jobs. The U.S. exports about $95 billion to the EC annually. The total annual U.S. exports throughout the world is only about 7 percent of the GNP. America's major trading partners export approximately 19 percent of their total GNPs.[1] In the next several years, there will be much political impetus to increase exports in order to secure trade parity, lower the trade deficit, and provide better-paying jobs. Under the prevailing wisdom, the U.S. government will do all it can to eliminate tariff and technical trade barriers that may impede free trade. And with a flat domestic consumption, there will be much more incentive to increase exports.

As well, the integration challenges encountered by the Europeans are an early warning of the challenges facing the U.S., Canada, and Mexico with the North American Free Trade Agreement (NAFTA).

---

[1] B. G. Simson, "Conformity Assessment Workshop on Electromagnetic Compatibility," Washington, D.C.: U.S. Department of Commerce, 1991, p. 3.

GOVERNMENT TO GOVERNMENT

Government today sits as an invisible partner of every company, every family, and every individual in the country.
—WILLIAM WEARLY, CEO,
International Division of Ingersoll-Rand

The Europeans are reluctant to accept certain U.S. mechanisms of conformity assessment, whether they are quality systems certification or product test data. To circumvent this problem, an American company planning to export to the EC must test its prototype by an EC laboratory or be certified by an EC registrar. Companies with a test facility or access to one in the EC can easily meet this requirement. However, the process is expensive and delays product introduction, which, in turn, hinders competitiveness. It is a hardship for medium and small manufacturers and independent laboratories. Finally, this practice could restrain trade. The EC Commission is encouraging governments to become involved in the conformity assessment of safety, health, consumer, and environmentally sensitive products.

NOTIFIED BODY STATUS

Because of the product-safety directives, EC-member states are responsible for determining the competence of test labs and certification bodies. The EC Commission is authorized to request information or can require verification of these laboratories' and certification bodies' qualifications and competence from member states, or third countries like the U.S. These groups must show compliance with a series of standards, EN 45000, which are discussed later in the chapter. Member states then notify their selections to the EC Commission.

MUTUAL RECOGNITION AGREEMENTS

Under the EC system, only member states can designate these notified bodies. But there's an exception. *To encourage free trade, countries outside of the EC can establish a Mutual Recognition Agreement (MRA) under which these third countries can authorize or certify notified bodies.* By extension, any nation has the similar right to request a trading partner to verify the competence and qualification of these groups. The purpose of this reciprocity is to ensure that EC members and trading partners have equal access and opportunities to certify through each other's quality systems and products.[2]

By negotiating national Mutual Recognition Agreements, individual nations would be responsible for establishing and maintaining their structure of testing and certification assurance. Each country certifies accreditors whose responsibility is to ensure the credibility of laboratories, quality systems registrars, and product testing facilities. Each country, including the U.S., ostensibly serves as guarantor of the integrity and competency of its notified bodies.

EC notified bodies could conceivably subcontract specific activities to extend their ability to perform testing activities outside the EC. The notified bodies would hold subcontractors to their own level of standards. Notified bodies would remain responsible for any subcontracted certification activity.

STEADY, BUT SLOW PROGRESS

A good deal of confusion still surrounds the conformity of quality systems, products, and the acceptance of test results from one country to another. The EC has initiated the effort to achieve global testing and certification transparency, probably by the end of the '90s. The goal is to have equal access for all parties to markets and certification approvals. Any third country would guarantee that its testing and certification bodies would conduct their affairs according to the Mutual Recognition Agreements.

The effort first starts with major industrial nations, newly industrialized countries, and finally the rest of the developing nations. Eventually, a global net of MRAs or similar understandings will be created whereby each country serves as a guarantor of its internal manufacturer's products.

Conceivably, "one stop" certification would allow the uninterrupted movement of products. Progress in setting up this structure has been slow in the EC and glacial in the rest of the world.

When these recognition agreements are established with the U.S. and other countries, then governments would be able to establish their own notified body structure. (A list of typical responsibilities of a U.S. notified body is shown on page 110.) This arrangement would create transparent and harmonized confor-

---

[2] International Trade Administration, "EC Testing and Certification Procedures Under the Internal Market Program, April 1, 1992, pp. 5–8.

Types of Responsibilities of U.S. Notified Bodies

1. Performs agreed tests, audits, inspections, and certifications required under the specified EC product directives for products originating and production processes located in the U.S. A U.S. notified body can only examine products that the manufacturer certifies are of U.S. origin. The U.S. notified body maintains a safety level at least equivalent to the EC's essential requirements.

2. Authorizes the manufacturer to affix the CE mark.

3. Cannot be the designer, manufacturer, supplier, or installer of the assessed product.

4. Maintains technical competence (ISO 9000, EN 45000, or equivalent) and professional integrity, free from pressures and inducement, particularly financial, which might influence judgment.

5. Has staff at its disposal and possesses the necessary facilities to enable it to perform and has access to the required equipment.

6. Agrees to U.S. government surveillance; for U.S. government to provide "assurance" to EC Commission of initial and ongoing technical competence; and to submit to U.S. government withdrawal of assurance and notified body status.

7. Agrees not to delegate any of its designated duties.

8. U.S. notified bodies are not obligated to reciprocate and accept certificates issued by EC notified bodies for compliance to U.S. requirements. U.S. authorities agree to recognize tests, audits, inspections, and certificates issued by selected European notified bodies for U.S. requirements covered by the same agreement.

9. Meets regularly with EC parties to handle issues.

10. Takes part in coordination meeting with EC Commission and their European counterparts.

Source: EC Commission, "Guidelines for Negotiation of Mutual Recognition Agreements with Third Countries," November 18, 1991, and "Commission Communication to the Council on the Negotiation of Agreements Between the EEC and Certain Third Countries on Mutual Recognition in Relation to Conformity Assessment," April 7, 1992.

mity assessment throughout the world. Companies would be able to test and certify products and quality systems in the U.S. that would be acceptable in the EC and in countries that have similar bilateral or multilateral agreements. The MRAs would probably be on an industry sector-by-sector basis, starting with EC safety directives, including telecommunications, pressure vessels, and electro-magnetic compatibility.[3]

EN 45000 Standards

EN 45000 standards address the following criteria with which accreditation and registration bodies must comply:

EN 45001   Criteria for Operation of Testing Laboratories

EN 45002   Criteria for Assessment of Testing Laboratories

EN 45003   Criteria for Operation of Accreditation Bodies

EN 45011   Criteria for Certification Bodies Operating Product Certification

EN 45012   Criteria for Certification Bodies Operating Quality Systems Certification

EN 45013   Criteria for Certification Bodies Operating Certification of Personnel

See page 117 for a discussion of these standards.

CONFORMITY ASSESSMENT SYSTEMS EVALUATION

The nine most terrifying words in the English language are: "I'm from the government and I'm here to help."
—RONALD REAGAN

Early in 1992, the National Institute of Standards and Technology (NIST) sought comments on a proposal to establish a Conformity Assessment Systems Evaluation (CASE) program. The Department of Commerce, acting through NIST, would assure the Europeans of the competence of U.S. conformity assessment bodies. NIST planned to offer a fee-based service in a voluntary program for

[3] "EC Commission Expects Mandate for MRAs Soon," Washington, D.C.: U.S. Department of Commerce, July–August, 1992, p. 4.

evaluating the competence of conformity assessment groups and provide official recognition of those qualifying. Conformance-based bodies would include quality system (ISO 9000) registration, product certification, and laboratory testing.

Why should the U.S. government become involved in what traditionally was a private-sector activity? The major reason is that the EC and other nations want to negotiate with national-level counterparts to ensure the credibility of any consumer, environmental, safety, or health conformity assessment mandated products entering the EC.

NIST expressed the rationale for the program as:

> The EC and the governments of other trading partners have indicated a desire to deal with a government entity which can provide assurance of the validity of U.S. conformity assessment activities pertaining to products regulated in foreign countries. To implement its regulations, the EC has established a harmonized conformity assessment approach based on notified bodies that are designated (notified) by a governmental body in each member state.[4]

THREE INVOLVEMENT LEVELS

NIST proposed three levels of conformity assessment:

Recognition level. NIST would recognize laboratory accreditation bodies, accreditors of certification bodies, and accreditors of registrars. Most U.S. standards stakeholders concur with this level of government involvement.

Accreditation level. NIST would accredit registration and certification bodies, including those conducting quality systems audits. This would be a normal extension since NIST is already accrediting testing laboratories through its National Voluntary Laboratory Accreditation Program (NVLAP). However, there seems to be wide objection among U.S. standards groups of this involvement level largely because it is perceived as intervention at the operating level where market decisions should prevail.

---

[4] Federal Register, "Request for Comments on a Proposal to Establish the Conformity Assessment Systems Evaluation (CASE) program, March 27, 1992, p. 10620.

Conformity level. NIST does not want to be involved at this level of quality system registration, product certification, or laboratory testing. For example, NIST does not see itself conducting audits, providing consulting, maintaining registers of companies, or conducting surveillance audits.

National Voluntary Laboratory Accreditation Program (NVLAP)

There is a precedent for government involvement. The National Voluntary Laboratory Accreditation Program, administered by NIST, is often offered as a successful example of U.S. government–sponsored conformity assessment.

NVLAP was established to accredit competent laboratories to perform a specific test or types of tests such as carpet testing, computer-applications testing, and construction-materials testing. Competence is defined as a laboratory's ability to meet the NVLAP conditions and to conform to specified criteria.

NVLAP technical experts, *peer assessors*, conduct on-site assessments and reviews. Upon correction of any deficiencies and approval by the assessors, NVLAP issues a certificate and defines the scope of laboratory accreditation. NVLAP accreditation criteria address quality systems, staff, facilities and equipment, calibration procedures, test methods, records, and test reports.

In general, the goals of NVLAP are:

- to provide national recognition for competent laboratories

- to provide laboratory management with a quality assurance check of laboratory performance

- to identify competent laboratories for use by regulatory agencies, purchasing authorities, and product certification systems

- to provide laboratories with guidance from technical experts to help them in reaching a higher level of performance

- to promote international acceptance of test data produced by NVLAP accredited laboratories

- to provide a technical basis for public- and private-sector certification programs

Source: "National Voluntary Laboratory Accreditation Program," NIST, Washington, D.C., 1992.

HARMONIZATION OF REGULATED AND NONREGULATED STANDARDS TO ISO 9000

Mutual recognition, as anticipated, will be completed on a sector-by-sector basis, first starting with regulated industries—those specifically addressed by an EC directive. The lead U.S. agencies in charge of the regulated areas will probably be the U.S. accrediting agency. For example, to ensure compliance of the Toy Directive, the Consumer Product Safety Commission can serve as the U.S. accreditor and the Food and Drug Administration can serve a similar function to ensure compliance with the Medical Devices Directive. There is a federal agency for most regulated products as the following explains:

Pressure Vessels Directive Compliance

If there isn't a federal agency directly responsible for an area (for example, construction products), NIST will probably serve as the lead organizing, coordinating, and accrediting agency. One area already fairly well addressed is pressure vessels, and the American Society of Mechanical Engineers (ASME) already has an auditing mechanism for assessing conformance to its requirements. It seems logical that the ASME quality control requirements are harmonized to ISO 9000. As well, it is fairly easy for the U.S. pressure vessels community to obtain consensus and unanimity so there is a good chance for EC reciprocity on ASME boiler and pressure vessels standards. This has been done by the Food and Drug Administration, which brought its Good Manufacturing Practices (GMP) regulations into harmony with ISO 9000 requirements.[5]

Toy Directive Compliance

Under the Consumer Product Safety Act, Congress granted the Consumer Product Safety Commission authority to issue and enforce product safety standards. These standards prescribe performance requirements, warnings, and instructions for the use of consumer products.

In anticipation of its conformity assessment involvement with the Toy Directive, CPSC is already recommending toy importers:

[5] B. G. Simson, "Conformity Assessment Workshop of Pressure Vessels," Washington, D.C.: U.S. Department of Commerce, 1991, p. 8.

ASME and CE Marks

For the last 100 years, one of the most widely adopted and recognized conformity assessment marks has been the American Society of Mechanical Engineers mark on pressure vessels, such as boilers. The mark is physically placed on the product.

The original benefit and continuing rationale for its use was that early train and manufacturing boilers were made to different specifications. Inconsistent boiler design, sloppy manufacturing, and abuse resulted in catastrophic explosions. ASME developed uniform rules for the design and manufacture of boilers. This mark was subsequently adopted internationally. Since the Pressure Vessels Directive requires specific conformity assessment and the attachment of the CE mark, it would be logical for ASME to seek notified status so that it could administer the CE mark in the U.S.

Source: B. G. Simson, "Conformity Assessment Workshop of Pressure Vessels," Washington, D.C.: U.S. Department of Commerce, 1991, p. 8.

- be aware of consumers' needs

- implement Total Quality Management Systems

- strongly consider third-party (ISO 9000) registration

- be aware of consumer complaints and have mechanisms to respond to them

- be an objective, safety-conscious company

- be aware of the new legislation by the U.S. Congress

- be familiar with individual state regulations[6]

[6] N. Steorts, "The U.S. Viewpoint on Product Safety and Quality: The Toy Industry," Vital Speeches, December 15, 1991, pp. 133–138.

REGISTRAR ACCREDITATION BOARD

A journey of a thousand miles must begin with a single step.
—CHINESE PROVERB

The Registrar Accreditation Board (RAB), an affiliate of the American Society for Quality Control (ASQC), is a private accreditation and certification initiative. *RAB seeks to create uniformity among U.S. third-party quality system certifiers, called* registrars, *in the regulated and nonregulated sectors.* Registration to ISO 9001/9002/9003 is gaining popularity as a condition of business for commercial customers as well as the perceived conformance of choice for regulated products in the EC and in the U.S.

RAB is governed by a board of directors from industry, academe, and consulting organizations. Its structure, mandate, procedures, and policies are patterned after its EC counterparts.[7]

JOINT ACCREDITATION

To present a unified and powerful front, in early 1992 the Registrar Accreditation Board and American National Standards Institute (ANSI) formed a joint accrediting venture. In late 1992 this relationship was extended through a Memorandum of Understanding to include the Dutch Raad voor de Certificate (RvC). In the memo of understanding ANSI-RAB and RvC would work toward recognizing each other's accreditation efforts.

This effort made eminent sense. RAB is an affiliate of the American Society for Quality Control, which chairs the U.S. Technical Advisory Group to ISO Technical Committee 176. This group, consisting of some seventy members, is often chosen from ASQC membership. ANSI is the official U.S. representative to ISO. RvC would have access to U.S. accreditors and the U.S. accreditors would have access to an EC-member-nation accreditor and through the EC mutual recognition principle to the EC in general.

[7] J. Stratton, "What Is the Registrar Accreditation Board?" Quality Progress, January 1992, pp. 67–69.

WHY RAB?

The question is often asked: Who appointed RAB to head up U.S. private accreditation? Well, the answer is probably that RAB appointed itself. There was a market need for U.S. conformity assessment, to provide value to U.S. manufacturers who wanted to do business in Europe. Someone had to do it. The marketplace abhors a vacuum. Why not RAB and ASQC? ASQC had the informed quality professionals who could supply the expertise and direction to initiate an accreditation effort.

Also, the possible unregulated proliferation of certifiers and quality auditors demanded that there be a mechanism similar to what EC-member nations were employing to accredit their certification bodies. It was believed the diversity of registrars and no formal mechanism for certifying quality auditors could deteriorate the infant U.S. certification process.

U.S. REGISTRAR QUALIFICATIONS

U.S. registrars must conform and follow procedures for registering companies and conducting audits similar to those of their European counterparts. All quality systems registrars and organizations maintaining the registers of manufacturing companies and conducting audits follow a program based on EN 45012, ISO Guide 48, and ISO 10011-2:

- EN 45012 deals with the "criteria for certification bodies operating quality systems certification." (A list of EN 4500 standards is shown on page 111.)

- ISO Guide 48 explains the "guidelines for third-party assessment and registration of a supplier's quality system."

- ISO 10011-2 spells out the qualifications and requirements that quality systems auditors must satisfy. (This standard is discussed in Chapter 8.)

EN 45012 is concerned with registrar certification. In the U.S., RAB accredits registrars, which are the companies that audit companies and maintain the supplier registers. RAB has adopted almost verbatim the requirements set out by EN 45012.

RAB requires the following from registrars:

- quality manual, quality systems, and procedures detailing how audits will be conducted; financial stability; and register maintenance

- completion of a number of ISO 9000 audits

- on-site audit by RAB

How Do Auditors Become Certified?

RAB has developed criteria that harmonize the training and experience of quality auditors to ISO 10011-2. Certification requires training in a RAB-approved course. The two paths to meet training requirements for auditor certification are a thirty-six-hour course that includes training in ISO 9000 series training, quality system audit training, communication abilities, and an examination of this material; or a sixteen-hour course and the American Society for Quality Control Certified Quality Auditor training.

Is Your Registrar Qualified?

This one basic question should be asked by all companies seeking registration. It is not an easy question because the answer is based on what is meant by "qualified." One type of qualification is that the registrar has been certified as a notified body for third-party assessments. The other question is: Who "notified" the registrar? These are important issues that are still being decided.

Many U.S. registrars establish their qualifications and credibility by arranging Memoranda of Understanding with other countries' certification bodies. Certification MOUs are agreements between two third-party certification groups, such as registrars, that state the level of mutual recognition of each other's certification. In terms of third-party certification, these levels of MOUs exist:

Basic MOU. This is an agreement between two organizations to discuss mutual recognition at some time in the future. This simply states that there is a working and mutual beneficial relationship between the two parties to agree to agree at some point in the future.

Evolving MOU. This agreement, sometimes called a *developing MOU*, implies the two parties have been working together for some time and trust has evolved.

EN 45012
General Criteria for Certification Bodies Operating
Quality System Certification

Contents

The scope and nature of EN 45012, a nine-page document, can be appreciated by its table of contents.

1. Object and field of application

2. Definitions

3. General requirements

4. Administrative structure

5. Terms of reference of governing board

6. Organizational structure

7. Certification personnel

8. Documentation and change control

9. Records

10. Certification and surveillance procedures

11. Certification and surveillance facilities required

12. Quality manual

13. Confidentiality

14. Publications

15. Appeals

16. Internal audit and periodic review

17. Misuse of certificates

18. Complaints

19. Withdrawal and cancellation of certificates

Each has agreed to assess the other's quality documentation, audit each other's organizations, and conduct joint audits of companies. The purpose is to continue building trust and confidence. In these often confidential documents, both parties share quality certificates, promote each other, conduct joint auditor training, meet regularly to share information, and agree to work to full bilateral MOU.

Full MOU. This agreement, sometimes called a bilateral agreement, means each party accepts the other party's quality reports, documentation, and certification results. This requires a high level of trust and confidence of the other party's credibility, consistency, and reliability.

Is Your Auditor Qualified?

Training courses that are recognized by RAB usually have the following wording: "This course is recognized by the Registrar Accreditation Board, a subsidiary of the American Society for Quality Control, and meets the training portion of the requirements for certification of Individual Provisional Auditors, Auditors, and Lead Auditors."[8] RAB stresses that the word *recognized* must be used. RAB or ASQC sponsorship is not stated or implied.

Problems Are Only Challenges Waiting to Be Solved

A major challenge with ISO 9000 is the lack of consistent interpretation of the ISO 9000 elements by quality systems auditors. "Auditors should not be using their whim to impose conditions that are not required on manufacturers," stated one anonymous ISO auditing authority. There is a valid concern that third-party auditors will add cost and little value to the customer-supplier relationship.

One way to create consistency among auditors is through auditor certification systems such as the one proposed by RAB. However, the level of history, success, precedent, and documentation does not rival financial or internal auditing. As more third-party registrar audits are conducted, the RAB or any other quality auditor certification will earn its trust and respect.

There is a mechanism for ensuring auditor consistency. The major mechanism

---

[8] Registrar Accreditation Board, "Requirements for Recognition of an Auditor Training Course," Milwaukee, WI: ASQC, 1992, p. 4.

of ensuring auditor reliability is through the complaint-and-feedback system that RAB has established to ensure that complaints are monitored, investigated, and corrected.

RATIONALE FOR GOVERNMENT INVOLVEMENT

Advocates of U.S. government and of private-sector involvement have publicly conflicted. The story is pretty much the same. A government agency is interjecting itself into private standards development.

One voice for limited U.S. government involvement was Amiram Daniel, director of Corporate Regulatory Affairs for Olympus Corporation and a member of the U.S. Technical Advisory Group to ISOTC 176 who said in a private discussion:

> Because of the pluralistic system of our standard-setting processes, not enough companies are heard from to fully justify the U.S. position as being truly representative. I, therefore, believe that some government coordinating role—not a supervisory or a standard-setting role—should be undertaken to ensure that the multitudes of companies and various areas of endeavors are truly representative in the quality dialogue and their concerns are represented in whatever position the U.S. undertakes."

RECOGNIZE ME, BUT STAY AWAY

The politics of U.S. conformity assessment can be distilled into the following: the Europeans want to negotiate nation-to-nation MRAs. The U.S. government or some other nation would authorize certification or testing efforts within its borders. NIST, in conjunction with other U.S. government agencies, would serve as facilitator or lead agency to negotiate the MRAs. While RAB and ANSI, both private organizations, have tried to position themselves as authoritative groups capable of negotiating with the Europeans, the Europeans have steadfastly ruled in favor of nation-to-nation agreements. The next best option for ANSI/RAB is to be recognized by the U.S. government. In other words, ANSI/RAB would like to be the accrediting body for the U.S. to provide the essential transparency, credibility, and harmony with Europe.

U.S. GOVERNMENT INVOLVEMENT

The U.S. government does have a role in the standards process. The U.S. government:

- can promote U.S. national consensus standards and conformity assessment programs for different industry sectors as a means to satisfy specific EC directives;

- can negotiate with the EC to provide an agreement to designate notified bodies for various U.S. industrial sectors;

- can establish sectoral Technical Advisory Committees to develop positions to be used in negotiating with the EC and other countries;

- is a large purchaser of products and services, and can provide direction to public-sector procurement;

- has the power to encourage the development of harmonized standards that will protect the public good;

- can mediate difficult, confusing, and conflicting agendas among U.S. standards-making groups;

- can certify and provide discipline for quality auditors and quality auditing;

- can represent and communicate U.S. business interests abroad;

- can identify and promote the need for international coordination in harmonization and conformity assessment;

- can work to ensure EC standards are not barriers to trade;

- can insist on technical transparency and harmony, including access to information and opportunities to influence standards development; and

- can maximize possibilities for testing and certification.

The next chapter discusses registrars and what the next level of the hierarchy does. The primary function of the registrars is to conduct third-party quality audits and to list approved companies in a register.

CHAPTER 7

Registrars and Quality Auditing

Incomprehensible jargon is the hallmark of a profession.
— KINGMAN BREWSTER, President of
Yale University

The quality audit is the process by which a company's quality systems and processes are evaluated to determine ISO 9000 compliance. This chapter looks at the role of the quality auditor, serving as the representative of the registrar, and the auditing process itself.

THE QUALITY AUDIT

It is better to light a candle than to curse the darkness.
— CHINESE PROVERB

One of ISO 9001's twenty series elements is quality auditing. Some quality authorities consider this the most important element of ISO 9000 because it serves as the ongoing mechanism of ensuring that quality systems are effectively and efficiently pursuing an organization's objectives.

There are three quality guideline documents for auditing quality systems with ISO 9000:

- ISO 10011-1 Part 1, Auditing

- ISO 10011-2 Part 2, Qualification Criteria for Auditors

- ISO 10011-3 Part 3, Managing Quality Programs

Part 1 describes basic quality auditing principles for planning, conducting, and documenting quality systems audits. Like ISO 9001, this standard is very general, so it can be applied to any industry, sector, system, process, or product. This remarkable strength is balanced by a major weakness in that this guideline has to be interpreted and tailored to the specific application.

Part 2 provides minimum, general guidelines for quality auditors to ensure that audits are conducted effectively and uniformly. Again, the guidelines are very general, covering education, training, experience, and personal attributes, and are open to interpretation, such as the required attribute that "auditor candidates should be open-minded, mature, possess sound judgment, analytical skills, tenacity, the ability to perceive situations in a realistic way."[1]

Part 3 explains how the audit process should be managed. The guidelines address suitability of team members, their consistency, training, audit reporting, confidentiality, and code of ethics.

What Is a Quality Audit?

Often, terms such as *quality systems audit, process quality audit*, and *service audit* are used interchangeably. These three types of audits are called *quality systems audits*, which are all-encompassing, referring to a quality evaluation of the organization, authorities, processes, procedures, products, personnel, and resources. Surveillance audit, however, has a distinct definition as specified in the registrar-certified companies' contracts. It is a periodic and announced audit to ensure that quality systems are in place and operating properly.

ISO 8402 defines *quality audit* as: "A systematic and independent examination

---

[1] ISO 10011-2, "Qualification Criteria for Auditors, Part 2," Geneva, Switzerland: International Organization for Standardization, p. 3.

to determine whether quality activities and related results comply with planned arrangements and whether these arrangements are implemented effectively and are suitable to achieve objectives."

WHY ARE ISO 9000 QUALITY AUDITS CONDUCTED?

A company may undergo multiple quality audits from existing and prospective customers. Each audit is expensive and time consuming. Wouldn't it make sense to undergo a single, widely accepted system assessment that would reduce the costs of multiple audits? ISO audits and registration are the method.

Quality auditing has recently come into its own. In the U.S., it has been widely used in the regulated industries dealing with nuclear, aviation, and medical devices. In the commercial sectors, quality audits have been used to evaluate, monitor, and correct suppliers.

Specifically, ISO 9000 quality audits are conducted to:

- evaluate compliance or conformance to customer's contractual requirements
- evaluate the effectiveness, efficiency, and economy of a company's operations
- pinpoint documentation problems
- increase operational understanding
- meet regulatory or other agency requirements
- allow an organization to become registered, as in ISO 9000 compliance
- determine corrective action or quality system effectiveness
- determine supplier certification levels, such as candidate, approved, or certified

ORGANIZATION OF THE AUDIT

Do everything you can do to avoid the appearance of wrong doing.
—JAMES POOLEY, Attorney

Who conducts the quality audits? What qualifications do these people need? How are the audits conducted? Let's start at the beginning.

There are three principals in a quality audit:

- client

- auditee—(the company)

- auditor

CLIENT'S RESPONSIBILITIES

The client is the organization requesting, authorizing, or paying for an audit. In a general quality audit, the client can be a customer that wants to audit suppliers, an organization wishing to audit itself, a regulatory body authorized to require product audits, or a third party assigned to list registering companies. In ISO auditing, the client and the auditee are often the same, usually a company seeking to be placed on a register of approved companies.

The client assumes some of the following responsibilities:

- authorizing the audit

- defining with the auditor audit requirements, scope, and timeliness

- appointing a representative to facilitate the audit

- providing facilities, phones, computers, and other resources to the auditor

- providing access to test results, measuring equipment, quality documentation, people, and processes

- reviewing audit information and results

- determining and authorizing actions to correct problems

- deciding on follow-up

AUDITOR'S RESPONSIBILITIES

The auditor is the person conducting the audit. If a team is performing the audit, the lead person is called the *lead auditor*. This person is sometimes called the *lead assessor*, if the person has been qualified by a European body.

Where are U.S. registrars obtaining their ISO quality auditors? Many are from the UK, where ISO 9000 and BS 5750 auditing has been around for years. Until recently, few U.S. auditors have had ISO 9000 auditing experience. Some have audited U.S. offshore plants and operations. Many were recruited from regulated industries in which they conducted military, nuclear, aerospace, or pharmaceutical industry quality audits. These are similar to ISO 9000 compliance audits.

Twenty Benefits of Quality Auditing

Internal and external quality auditing are considered important Total Quality Management assessment tools. In general, internal quality auditing can be used for the following:

1. verify conformance with quality standards, engineering drawings, specifications, and regulatory requirements

2. establish quality baselines

3. measure improvements

4. maintain competitiveness by benchmarking world-class competitors

5. identify and reduce liability exposure

6. ensure external and internal customer satisfaction

7. improve internal operations

8. measure and monitor quality program effectiveness

9. measure and report process efficiency and effectiveness

10. monitor continuous improvement

11. set and measure benchmark attainment

12. monitor product quality

13. comply with contractual requirements

14. monitor personnel effectiveness

15. monitor and measure supplier improvement

16. establish performance baselines

17. evaluate and measure service quality

18. identify areas for corrective action

19. identify areas for quality improvement

20. improve financial performance.

Source: G. Hutchins, *Quality Auditing* (Englewood Cliffs, NJ: Prentice Hall, 1992), pp. 28–29.

The lead auditor is the person with the authority and responsibility to plan, conduct, and report audit results. In an ISO 9000 audit, the lead auditor requests the assistance of the auditee's organization in conducting the audit. The lead auditor has several other important functions, specifically:

- selecting the audit team

- representing the team to the customer and auditee

- organizing the audit team

- being responsible for the final report

- identifying and defining the customer's requirements

- examining quality documentation

- planning the audit

- managing the audit

- presenting audit results to the customers

THREE STAGES OF A QUALITY AUDIT

If you get all the facts, your judgment can be right; if you don't get all the facts, it can't be right.
—BERNARD BARUCH

A quality audit can be divided into three stages:

- Audit Planning

- Audit Implementation

- Audit Reporting/Closure

AUDIT PLANNING

The mark of a professional quality auditor is the ability to plan so time is not wasted and operations are not disrupted. The client makes the final determination of the quality systems that are to be audited. These are usually specified in a

---

What Makes a Good Quality Auditor?

You cannot create experience. You must undergo it.
—ALBERT CAMUS

The following are requisite skills of a quality auditor:

- professional proficiency
- due professional care
- sufficient knowledge and skills
- knowledge of quality standards and systems
- flexibility
- people skills
- communication skills
- temperament
- diligence
- analytical skills
- critical attitude

Source: G. Hutchins, *Quality Auditing* (Englewood Cliffs, NJ: Prentice Hall, 1992), p. 35.

---

contract, purchase order, or quality standard. In the case of ISO 9000, the quality standard spells out audit scope, requirements, and quality systems elements.

The frequency of audits is determined by the registrar. There may be bi-yearly surveillance audits and recertification audits every three years. As well, major quality system changes may necessitate an audit.

The Lead Auditor

Depending on the scope and complexity, the audit may be conducted by one person or a team. *Usually, at least one person on the audit team has specific experience in the industry being assessed.*

A lead auditor is in charge of planning, organizing, and reporting audit results.

Eighteen Key Characteristics of Internal Quality Auditing

Internal quality auditing is exploding. It is seen as one of the major mechanisms for continuous improvement. The following are key characteristics of quality auditing in the 1990s:

1. external customer satisfaction

2. internal customer satisfaction

3. participatory problem solving

4. systematic appraisal

5. identification and minimization of risks

6. objective and independent appraisal

7. efficiently, effectively, and economically used resources

8. achievable organizational objectives

9. relevant, accurate, and reliable information

10. knowledge of diverse operations and functions

11. compliance to quality standards

12. degree of correspondence

13. internal control monitoring

14. understandable and usable communicated results

15. corrective action

16. company-wide and supplier-wide continuous improvement

17. prevention orientation

18. technical and statistical orientation

Source: G. Hutchins, *Quality Auditing* (Englewood Cliffs, NJ: Prentice Hall, 1992), p. 5.

In general, the lead auditor is the main contact person on the audit team before, during, and after the audit. Being lead auditor also implies the person has fulfilled experience, training, testing, and auditing certification requirements.

The lead auditor is often certified by an accrediting agency such as RAB, through education and training. Lead auditors are often full-time employees of the registrar. Other auditors on the team may be contract or part-time workers. Registrars will use full-time employees to manage audits or conduct surveillance or reaudits during off periods. Registrars, especially recently with the tremendous increase in audit activity, are hiring contractors to be part of a team to conduct specialized or complex audits and to smooth out the peaks in audit activity.

AUDIT IMPLEMENTATION

> *Information may be accumulated files, but it must be retrieved to be of use in decision making.*
> —KENNETH ARROW, Economist

How does the auditor confirm conformance to the applicable ISO 9000 standard? Many quality auditors have conducted MIL-Q 9858A audits in regulated industries such as aerospace, medical devices, or nuclear. These audits are similar to ISO audits. ISO audits are essentially compliance audits in which the auditor first ensures the auditee addresses all of the ISO requirements then seeks corroboration that what is stated in the quality documentation is actually done.

ISO has developed generic guidelines, addressed in ISO 9000-2 for the application of ISO 9001, ISO 9002, and ISO 9003. While these are primarily for internal use, the guidelines offer the auditor broad guidance on how the guidelines can be implemented. The auditor should still have specific industry background to fully understand how each specific guideline should be implemented.

To illustrate how the guide addresses the first ISO 9001 systems element, Management Responsibility, the company seeking registration is required to define and document quality policy, objectives, and commitments. The auditor would ensure that quality policies are easy to understand and relevant to the organization and that quality objectives are ambitious and achievable.[2]

---

[2] "Quality Management and Quality Assurance Standards, Part 2: Generic Guidelines for the Application of ISO 9001, ISO 9002, and ISO 9003," Geneva, Switzerland: International Organization for Standardization, 10011-2, p. 2.

"Show Me"

In an ISO audit, management is not the final arbiter of who and what will constitute compliance with an ISO element. Previously, especially in customer-supplier audits, the auditor and the company's management and technical representatives would spend much of the audit in a closed room reviewing data to determine compliance. The auditor would accept management's guarantee that quality was being pursued. Now there is more a "show me" and "prove it" auditor mentality. The auditor goes on the line or to an area to determine conformance and interview line personnel to determine if they follow procedures. The auditor does not want the supervisor or process engineer coaching these people.

What Is the Auditor Really Looking For?

> *Intelligence from the source is much more useful than laundered reports.*
>
> —JOHN R. WHITNEY, Educator

In an ISO 9000 quality systems audit, *the auditor first determines if quality documentation, usually the quality manual, addresses the ISO quality elements.* Then, the auditor will visit a site and collect and analyze evidence to verify the quality system controls described in the quality documentation are in place and are operating properly. For example, verification may mean the auditor interviews people on the line or directly observes operations. But the important point to emphasize is that *audits are fundamentally subjective.* An auditor may interpret a particular ISO 9000 clause differently than another auditor and each may have a different philosophy. And, there may be a number of ways to indicate conformance. Some auditors may require more or less systematic procedures, or conformance may be indicated through training with a reduced emphasis on procedures. As well, there is no universally accepted audit system to follow. For example, should procedures and quality documentation detail all activities, or should documentation be more general?

Two Critical Quality Systems

There are twenty quality system elements in ISO 9001. Which are the most important? Having spoken to a number of quality auditors, probably the two most often checked quality system requirements in full and surveillance audits are *Internal Auditing* and *Corrective Action*.

There are several excellent reasons for close scrutiny of both areas. First, quality audits are snapshots of operations; one look every six months at a complex operation does not provide a clear view of what is happening on a daily basis. On the other hand, the auditor can check the results of internal audits and the effectiveness of corrective actions. The internal audits supply a view of what transpired since the last audit. As well, a review of the corrective actions reveals if problems recurred. If they haven't, then it shows that quality systems are in place, working properly, and hopefully quality is improving.

In a discussion with Gary Lewis, director of Quality Systems for Amoco Performance Products and a member of the U.S. TAG to ISO/TC 176, he emphasized the importance of internal auditing:

> Supervisors and managers have to be made accountable for implementing and measuring—(self-evaluating)—the quality system activities in their own area and to give feedback to senior management. Remember, the ISO program manager or designated ISO representative can only orchestrate—(facilitate)—the quality system process. It is the supervisors and managers who have to implement and use the system.

Questionnaires

> *Without a yardstick, there is no measurement. And without measurement, there is no control.*
> —PRAVIN SHAH, Management
> Consultant

Most quality auditors use questionnaires to plan and conduct quality audits. The registrar has specialized questionnaires for different industries and their specialized processes and functions. For example, the registrar may have questionnaires for quality assurance, purchasing, engineering, and manufacturing areas in chemical process industries.

The auditor also can request the company's quality documentation, which may be incorporated into a quality manual. The auditor checks the major sections of the manual against the appropriate ISO 9000 criteria. Then, the auditor or team develops questions from the ISO standard and tailors them to the auditee's documentation. The questionnaire has three response choices—Yes, No, or NA (Not Applicable)—and a documentation column. *Yes* or *NA* responses require no action. A *No* response requires further investigation or corrective action. The documentation column refers to the customer's supporting documentation that applies to the question.

Determining "What Is" Against "What Should Be"

To obtain evidence to make a reasonable decision, the quality auditor assesses "what is" being done against "what should be" as it is spelled out in the quality manual. Methods may include observing quality tests; interviewing personnel; analyzing and evaluating inspection documents, work instructions, prototypes, reliability tests, and contracts and purchase orders; verifying engineering calculations and written representations; and investigating field failures.[3]

Hierarchical Quality Manuals

Quality documentation is often hierarchical. There are many types of quality documentation, such as company policies, operating procedures, work instructions, engineering drawings, process flow diagrams, and product specifications. A commonly used hierarchy consists of three levels:

First level. This usually consists of the quality manual. The organization defines its company quality policies according to the specific ISO 9000 quality requirements.

Second level. This level consists of operating procedures that define what has to be done and those responsible for ensuring it.

Third level. This level consists of work instructions of how things are done to conform to quality requirements of the second level. For example, if there are recurring problems, this level documentation would specify how corrective action fixes the problem and eliminates its recurrence.[4]

---

[3] G. Hutchins, *Quality Auditing* (Englewood Cliffs, NJ: Prentice Hall, 1992), pp. 110–11.

[4] G. Loftgren, "Quality System Registration," Milwaukee, WI: ASQC—Registration Accreditation Board, 1991.

What Does the Quality Auditor Look For?

Facts are friendly.
— IRWIN MILLER, Former CEO,
Cummins Engine Co.

Regardless if the auditor is from Switzerland or the U.S., the quality auditor basically follows the same procedure for determining compliance to ISO 9000. The following are some of the critical ISO 9001 quality system elements that a Swiss Association for Quality Certificates (the registrar) auditor may look for when conducting an ISO 9001 audit:

Section 1: Management Responsibility

- Top management developed and supports quality policy.

- Management is familiar with quality policies.

- Top management person is responsible for quality.

- Top management person periodically assesses quality system.

- Quality responsibilities, authorities, and interrelationships are defined.

Section 2: Quality Systems

- Quality systems are described in quality handbooks or manuals.

- Quality documentation reflects ISO requirements.

- Knowledge of quality systems is appropriate to the organizational level and function.

Section 3: Contract Review

- All contracts are reviewed for ability to meet requirements.

- Quality-relevant features are identified in contracts.

(*continued on the following page*)

What Does the Quality Auditor Look For? (*continued*)

- Production or other procedures are developed to meet contract requirements.

- Contract-review records are maintained.

Section 4: Design Control

- Design procedures are developed.

- Design plans identify responsibilities, timelines, budgets, etc.

- Technical design interfaces are identified.

- Design input requirements are identified.

- Designs are reviewed and approved by appropriate parties.

- Design modifications are reviewed and approved by appropriate parties.

Section 5: Document Control

- All quality documents are reviewed and approved.

- Document production, verification, approval, distribution, and filing is controlled.

- Document amendments are reviewed and approved.

- Master list of modified documents is maintained.

Section 6: Purchasing

- Supplied products satisfy requirements.

- Purchasing documents are accurate, complete, and current.

- Suppliers are selected and monitored based on their ability to satisfy customer requirements.

- Assessment criteria are identified.

- Supplied products are inspected and/or tested.

What Does the Quality Auditor Look For? (*continued*)

Section 7: Purchaser-Supplied Products

- Purchased products are stored and handled properly.
- Nonconforming products are segregated, and supplier is informed of their condition.

Section 8: Product Identification and Traceability

- Products are identified throughout production.
- Unique products or batches are tagged.

Section 9: Process Control

- Documentation defines process requirements.
- Production and installation requirements are defined and controlled.
- Production and installation processes are approved.
- Special processes are monitored and controlled.
- Production personnel are qualified.

Section 10: Inspection and Testing

- Incoming materials are inspected and/or tested.
- In-process materials are inspected and/or tested.
- Before released for delivery, final products are inspected and/or tested.
- Inspection and testing documents are accurate, complete, and current.
- Documents are available for review.

Section 11: Inspection, Measuring, and Testing Equipment

- Inspection, measuring, and testing equipment are controlled.
- Measurability and accuracy of equipment are ensured.

(*continued on the following page*)

What Does the Quality Auditor Look For? (*continued*)

- All measuring equipment is identified.
- Measuring equipment is referenced to international and national standards.

Section 12: Inspection and Testing Status

- Inspection and/or testing status of products is positively identified.
- Status records are accurate, complete, and current.

Section 13: Control of Nonconforming Products

- Nonconforming products are positively identified.
- Nonconforming product disposition is defined.
- Nonconforming products are reworked, accepted, or scrapped.
- Rejected products are disposed of properly.

Section 14: Corrective Action

- Causes of nonconforming products are systematically analyzed.
- Preventive measures are instituted to eliminate nonconformances.
- Efficacy of corrective action is analyzed.

Section 15: Handling, Storage, Packaging, and Delivery

- Internal transport movements are identified.
- Handling, storage, packaging, and delivery damage are minimized.
- Stored materials are systematically and periodically assessed.
- Material packaging effectiveness is assessed.
- Materials are protected during delivery.

What Does the Quality Auditor Look For? (*continued*)

Section 16: Quality Records

- Records are properly identified, maintained, filed, and indexed.
- Personnel are assigned for record maintenance.
- Records are traceable to a process or product.
- Retention and location of records are determined.

Section 17: Internal Quality Audits

- Periodic, comprehensive internal quality audits are conducted.
- Auditors are qualified.
- Audits follow a process of planning, implementation, and reporting.
- Auditors use comprehensive checklists that reflect customer requirements.
- Corrective action effectiveness is monitored.

Section 18: Training

- Training needs are periodically assessed.
- Training personnel are qualified.
- Training records are accurate, complete, and current.

Section 19: Servicing

- Servicing scope is identified.
- Servicing meets customer requirements.

Section 20: Statistical Techniques

- Statistical techniques are used when required.
- Statistical effectiveness is analyzed.

Source: T. Zahner, "Quality Assurance Certificates: How, Where and Why," Zurich, Switzerland: Swiss Association for Quality Assurance Certificates, 1991.

AUDIT REPORTING/CLOSURE

> *It is much harder to ask the right question than it is to find the right answer to the wrong question.*
>
> —E. E. MORRISON, Writer

The client receives the audit report, and it may state that everything is satisfactory. If the report indicates that stated ISO requirements are not being met, *the difference between "what is" and "what should be" (as specified by ISO requirements) is variously called findings, nonconformities, nonconformances, noncompliances, discrepancies, or deficiencies as noted.* The issues red-flagged become action items for correction.

The auditor initiates a Corrective Action Request (CAR) to fix the symptom and remove the root cause. The CAR points out the deficiency but does not reveal how it should be fixed. Corrective action is not the role of an auditor. The CAR, however, should be factual. The auditor should report nonconformances and not report specific recommendations for corrective action.

The request for corrective action can come from the customer or auditor, depending on the purpose of the audit. If a company is going through third-party registration, the auditor informs the customer, the company seeking registration, of the required corrective actions. If the customer purchases products from the supplier, the customer, through purchasing or quality assurance, will inform the supplier of corrective actions.

Most Common Auditing Deficiencies

Lack of document control and design control are the two most cited system discrepancies in conforming to ISO 9001 in Europe. The same probably holds true for the U.S. They involve not having all the relevant documents, such as workmanship standards, available at a work location or the use of outdated standards and regulations.

The sidebar on page 141 lists the percentage of ISO 9001 system discrepancies among the twenty system elements. The section numbers of ISO 9001 requirements are shown on the first column. To determine what each section refers to, consult the Sample Quality Manual in the appendix for details.

Closure

The audit report may indicate a number of discrepancies or deficiencies. Depending on the registrar or auditor, they may be prioritized in terms of critical, major, or minor. A critical discrepancy deals with health or safety issues; a major discrepancy with functional issues; and a minor discrepancy with cosmetic issues.

The audit is considered open, and registration withheld until a corrective action plan has been developed and implemented for each discrepancy. Depending on the process or product discrepancy and its severity, a post audit may be conducted.

Percentages of ISO 9001 System Discrepancies		
Section Number	*Title*	*Percent Nonconformity*
4.5	Document Control	18
4.4	Design Control	12
4.6	Purchasing	9
4.10	Inspection/Testing	8
4.2	Quality System	7
4.9	Process Control	6
4.11	Inspection/Measuring/Test Equipment	6
4.3	Contract Review	5
4.14	Corrective Action	4
4.1	Management Responsibility	4
4.16	Quality Records	4
4.15	Handling/Storage/Packaging/Delivery	4
4.17	Internal Quality Audits	4
4.18	Training	3
4.12	Inspection/Test Status	2
4.13	Control of Nonconforming Product	2
4.8	Product Identification/Traceability	2
4.19	Servicing	~0
4.20	Statistical Techniques	~0
4.7	Purchaser Supplied Products	~0

Source: Adapted from *Journal of European Business*, "Percentage of System Discrepancies Among 1,040 Nonconforming ISO 9001 Conditions."

CURRENT STATE OF QUALITY AUDITING

The buck stops here.
—HARRY S TRUMAN

Quality auditing is in a state of flux. Many issues discussed in this section will probably be resolved in the near future. However, at present they are causing problems in terms of the credibility of the ISO registration process.

QUALITY AUDITING IS RELATIVELY YOUNG

Quality auditing is still in its infancy. It does not have the history, trust, or respect as the Certified Public Accounting or Internal Auditing professions. Accounting audits, despite the recent S&L problems, are more established with well-codified auditing standards, an enforceable code of ethics, and an accepted certification program. It is just a matter of time before quality auditing develops this level of standard certification.

An example of acceptance of quality auditing and its predecessors can be seen in their reporting relationships. Quality auditors often report to a manager or director in the quality, engineering, or purchasing department. Sometimes, the head of quality auditing is a director, but more often a manager. On the other hand, the internal audit department usually reports to the audit committee of the board of directors. It's only when the benefits, needs, and requirements of quality auditing are fully appreciated that its importance will increase.

ISO 9000—OPEN TO INTERPRETATION

The quality auditor checks compliance or noncompliance to specific elements in the applicable ISO 9000 series, 9001/9002/9003.

The auditor may take a loose or strict interpretation of the ISO requirement as well as the method by which it is being complied. In some cases, the auditor may not be familiar with the auditee's industry, quality system, process, or products. In a large audit, one person should have experience in the particular industry being audited.

If there is a deficiency or other nonconformance, the quality auditor issues a

Corrective Action Request. The auditor, through corrective action, does not recommend a specific course of action. The registrar and auditor defer to the auditee to know what is best to remedy or correct the situation.

FEW BARRIERS TO ENTRY

A major problem with the entire ISO 9000 registration process is auditor quality. There are few barriers to becoming an ISO 9000 quality systems auditor. A widespread complaint from companies seeking registration is the lack of industry-, process-, and product-specific experience displayed by auditors. Often, conducting quality audits of sophisticated operations requires operational, technical, and product expertise. Companies are saying auditors don't have the required background. Registrars respond that the registration queue, the wait, is already so long that they can't find qualified people to train as auditors. In one case, a company complained that the auditor was technically incompetent. The auditor, two months prior, had been conducting empowerment training and now was being asked to evaluate complex technical processes and quality systems.

Several scenarios can be anticipated. The government develops guidelines for qualifying auditors. This is unlikely because of the bent toward self-regulation. At this time, several public groups are self-certifying and training auditors to conduct industry-, process-, or product-specific audits.

INTERNAL AND EXTERNAL AUDITORS

Quality audits are conducted by in-house auditors and external contractors. In-house auditors are full-time employees of the registrar. They often have multiple responsibilities, especially in small registrars, such as marketing, auditing, managerial, and administrative. Since they are full-time employees, they can communicate the registrar's policies, commitment, and procedures to prospective and existing customers, thereby increasing the confidence in the audit.

A registrar may retain external contractors for audits that require special expertise or if there is a sudden peak in audit activity. These people may be on retainer or used on a contract basis. They often have extensive auditing experience and are well known to the registrar. However, the quality level of external auditors can vary extensively. It's important for the registrar to vouch and be accountable for all auditors.

AUDITORS DON'T RUN BUSINESSES

A company decides what makes good business sense, then defines its requirements, policies, and procedures. The quality systems auditor assesses the company against what it is doing or says it is doing in complying to ISO quality systems. ISO 9001/9002/9003 leaves it up to companies to interpret the standard. *Auditors should not be using the guide to explicitly tell customers how to run their businesses.*

LITIGATION EXPOSURE

Two things will occur unless the issue of auditor qualification is resolved. Auditors conducting poor-quality audits will place the entire conformity assessment structure at risk. Conformity assessment is based on trust starting at the top, at the international and national level, and progressing down to the accreditor, registrar, and auditor level. If the lowest element of the structure, the quality of the auditor, is suspect, the top is not credible.

The second major problem is the exposure to audit risk, including auditor gross negligence and fraud. The following scenario can be imagined. A registrar approves and lists a supplier of critical products. A product fails, a death occurs, and the critical questions arise: Who is at fault and liable? Who pays and how much? This scenario is all too real with the scarcity of trained auditors assessing regulated industries.

DO AUDITS ADD VALUE?

It should be emphasized that ISO quality systems audits are compliance audits. In other words, the auditors ensure that all elements of the particular ISO standard are covered and that they verify conformance. The decision is binary, conforming/nonconforming, acceptable/unacceptable, and so on. The question to be asked: Are quality audits adding value to the business process?

If direct value cannot be attributed to ISO registration, the following could occur: A company will expend effort, time, and money becoming registered. However, the quality systems are not improved and maintaining registration becomes a bureaucratic effort to simply appease the registrar's auditors.

In the next chapter, we will look at a company seeking registration. We'll address the important issues that you will need to know about becoming registered in the most efficient, effective, and economical way.

CHAPTER 8

How to Become Registered

Knowing is not enough; we must apply. Willing is not enough, we must do.

— Johann von Goethe

This is probably the most important chapter in the book for those thinking of becoming registered. It's basically a hands-on guide to ISO registration.

The suggestions in this book were distilled through many conversations with professionals and represent their total wisdom. Some consultants tell their clients that if a similar program is followed, they will guarantee their registration. Unfortunately, I can't unequivocally make the same promise.

Companies pursuing ISO 9000 registration follow a logical, systematic three-stage process:

1. Preregistration—getting one's house in order

2. Registration—actual process of being audited and registered

3. Postregistration—process to maintain registration

PREREGISTRATION

Plan your work and work your plan.
—ANONYMOUS

Probably the most important stage is preregistration. It's during this stage that an applicant company understands what needs to be done and develops action plans for complying with each quality system.

ISO 9000 registration should be seen as a business decision. Many times, a company pursues quality registration as a means to garner business or to appease a customer. While these are important reasons, *the most important reason to pursue registration is to improve business systems, procedures, and operations.*

There are no hard and fast rules for becoming ISO 9000 registered. The following are common-sense suggestions that have worked for many successful companies:

1. Understand globalization of business

2. Talk to customers

3. Benchmark competition

4. Understand ISO 9000 standards and guidelines

5. Talk with stakeholders

6. Obtain top-management support

7. Establish a team

8. Attend a certification seminar

9. Develop a project schedule, plan, and estimate

10. Retain an ISO 9000 consultant

11. Conduct a preassessment

12. Upgrade quality documentation

13. Overcome obstacles and resistance

14. Evaluate internal quality systems

UNDERSTAND GLOBALIZATION OF BUSINESS

Effective management means asking the right questions.
—ROBERT HELLER, *US* editor

It's important for your company to understand trends in global technical standardization and conformity assessment specific to your industry and business. A broad-based view of your business should go beyond the technical nature of ISO 9000 registration. The overarching issue is to understand the greater context of ISO registration as a trade issue and as a business requirement to enter certain markets.

It's important to ask:

- Are countries or national standards organizations in which you want to market adopting global conformity assessment, testing, and harmonization standards?

- Are countries specifically adopting ISO 9000 standards?

- Is registration a condition to entry?

- Are new technical standards being developed?

- If yes, how are they different from current ones?

- What are the mechanisms for indicating laboratory and testing conformity?

The global trading system is in a state of flux due to harmonization of technical standards and to acceptance of conformity assessment mechanisms. ISO 9000 will probably emerge as the most commonly used approach to ensure conformity.

We've discussed specific EC directives. The Europeans and other countries are developing laws, standards, or other regulations that affect many industries and companies. More will be developed dealing with the environment, packaging, labeling, and product disposal. To ensure compliance, these will probably follow similar conformity assessment procedures as have been discussed.

TALK TO CUSTOMERS

Customers or perhaps customers' customers will probably provide the initial impetus and drive for ISO 9000 registration. A customer may require it to comply with its supplier-customer certification or with national or regulatory requirements, or to seek assurance that quality controls exist.

Registration is expensive. Many companies, especially small businesses down the supplier chain, have a parochial view of globalization. If it isn't required immediately to satisfy the customer, top management will inevitably ask: So why should this expense be incurred now? The main reason for ISO 9000 registration is simple: customers are requiring it. If registration is a line-item requirement in a contract or purchase order, then a company may have little choice. Registration then becomes a condition of business.

Important Questions to Ask

What should be done if:

- Only one customer requires registration?

- A customer two tiers away requires registration?

- A customer requires a specific mark?

- Customers and competitors are seeking registration?

- Federal agencies are soliciting comments for rule making?

- A customer harmonizes an existing quality standard to ISO 9000?

What happens if a company has ten customers and only one insists on registration? Chances are, most companies in an industry sector sooner or later will require it.

Or, what happens if a manufacturer requires all of its suppliers to become registered, even those two or more tiers away? In this case the answer is more difficult. If the customers' customer requires it, there is a good chance it will be pushed through the supplier chain. How soon? There is no easy answer. However, to be on the safe side, ask customers, their customers, and so on up the supplier chain what their immediate and future ISO registration plans are.

A company should ask the customer: Whose registration mark will you accept and why? This requires that a company understand what the Europeans and their customers are doing with conformity assessment. Not all registration marks are created equal. Some are better—more credible—than others.

A company should also understand its industry's and customer's competitive position. For example, if a company sells health-care and safety products that the Europeans have targeted with a specific directive, then it is almost certain that registration should be sought. Also, if most customers and competitors are similarly seeking registration, then it's also a safe bet a company will have to do the same. Customers may impose it as a contractual business requirement. Competitors will use it for competitive positioning.

Another indicator is the amount of interest a federal agency may have on the issue. The Department of Defense, the Food and Drug Administration, the Consumer Products Safety Commission, and others have sponsored seminars and have solicited comments in the Federal Register for proposed rule making. This activity indicates early warning signs that interest is building until a political consensus is achieved for it to become mandatory.

ISO 9000 registration may well be incorporated into existing supplier-certification efforts. Many programs have existed for years. Two of the better known are General Motors's Targets of Excellence and Ford's Q-101. Recently, both have incorporated elements of the Malcolm Baldrige National Quality Award. Conceivably, ISO 9000 may be incorporated into commercial supplier-certification programs. In these programs, a supplier is audited and, based on a numerical score, awarded candidate, approved, certified, or partnership status.

BENCHMARK COMPETITION

> *First we will be the best, and then we will be first.*
> —GRANT TINKER, Television Executive

Understand and benchmark your competition in regard to conformity assessment strategies. Is your competition pursuing ISO registration, seeking a product type certification, or seeking to be self-certified? In a rapidly changing global marketplace, standing still is the equivalent to moving backwards. A company may think that registration is too expensive or doesn't affect them. However, the competition may already be pursuing registration, which may put your company at a competitive disadvantage.

Reactive or Proactive Strategies

Your strategy may be reactive or proactive. Both offer some advantages. A reactive strategy involves seeking registration or some form of certification only when a customer or regulatory authority requires it. Registration is expensive and time consuming. Waiting until it's required makes sense. As we discussed, MRA, accreditation, registration, and auditor issues are still unresolved.

Another tactic is to become proactive. Farsighted companies, such as Du Pont, White-Rodgers, Hewlett-Packard, Beckman Instruments, Kodak, and others, are taking a proactive stance to ISO 9000 registration. The following scenario is occurring in many industries. Domestic growth is stagnant as offshore markets grow. ISO 9000 is becoming a necessary condition of business in these growth markets. Many executives take the view that it makes good business sense to be one of the first in an industry to become registered and use ISO 9000 to self-promote their commitment to quality and customer satisfaction. Early indicators of this trend can be seen in self-promoting ads in a variety of trade journals.

UNDERSTAND ISO 9000 STANDARDS AND GUIDELINES

Many companies seek registration without fully understanding the ISO 9000 standard and the other options of having products certified. By referring to the sample Quality Manual in the appendix, the scope of the standards can be appreciated. However, I strongly recommend that you purchase the entire set of ISO 9000 and 10011 standards. (The complete set can be purchased through the American Society for Quality Control [ASQC] or the American National Standards Institute [ANSI]. The addresses and phone numbers of these organizations are in the Resources section.)

The three major customer-supplier quality standards are ISO 9001, ISO 9002, and ISO 9003. They indicate what must be done to comply. The other ISO 9000 standards are guidance documents. Familiarity with these is recommended because they indicate what may be incorporated into future ISO 9000 revisions.

ISO 10011 series, covered on page 124, outlines what quality auditors do in planning, conducting, and reporting the registration audit results.

TALK WITH STAKEHOLDERS

Talk with people in the registration community: accreditors, registrars, auditors, and others. A partial list of stakeholders in the certification process includes customers, suppliers, management, employees, trade/industry groups, governmental agencies, and ISO consultants/auditors.

There is much activity, information, and resources surrounding ISO registration in the U.S., EC, and around the world. It's imperative to track ISO 9000, conformity assessment, and technical-standard developments that may affect a company.

What's the best way to do this? Consider the following:

- retaining an ISO consultant

- retaining a trade consultant

- participating in a trade/industry group

- participating with a standards organization

- subscribing to a newsletter

The Resources section of this book lists major U.S. and international players in the ISO 9000 arena. Stay on top of developments and act upon changes that may affect you.

Trade or Industry Group Participation

One of the more important groups with which to participate is an industry trade organization. If you want to market or produce products in the EC, there may be special testing and certification requirements that can be a trade barrier. Do you need different certificates from different member states for the same product? One way to find out what is going on and to participate in the process is to work with a trade association, preferably at the national and international levels.

Most regulated groups have been actively involved in the international testing and certification areas. For example, the Health Industry Manufacturers Association (HIMA) represents the interests of the medical devices industry; the National Electrical Manufacturers Association (NEMA) does the same in the electrical industry; and the American Society of Mechanical Engineers (ASME) closely follows pressure vessel developments. These groups often communicate and collaborate with their counterparts in other countries.

OBTAIN TOP-MANAGEMENT SUPPORT

Management's job is to see the company not as it is . . . but as it can become.

—JOHN TEETS, Chairman,
Greyhound Corp.

Once market requirements of registration and the standard specifics are understood, internal management support should be pursued. ISO 9000 specifically requires that a manager or representative be appointed with the authority and responsibility for ensuring that ISO 9000 is properly implemented and maintained. This person will work with the registrar and with internal groups to develop and document quality systems. Once systems are developed, this person is responsible for ensuring the proper maintenance of the quality systems.

A vice president or higher-level executive should champion the ISO 9000 registration effort. The standard itself requires the company's management "define and document its policy and objective for commitment to quality." The standard also requires that management continuously monitor and review quality system effectiveness. Questions to ask are:

- Is there the political and management will to pursue registration?

- Has a key champion for registration been identified?

- Does the company have a quality program?

- How will ISO registration be incorporated into the existing quality program?

- Does the organization have a quality culture?

- Is quality documentation sufficient for ISO registration?

Registration should not be perceived as an expedient to appease a customer or as another program that can be grafted onto the organization. There is a tendency to assume that registration is quick and easy.

ISO 9000 registration also involves a vertical and horizontal organizational change. As ISO 9000 implementation is pursued, resistance and objections may appear. Questions will arise. Why are we doing this? What is the purpose and value of this effort? And so on. Top management should actively support and demonstrate its commitment to ISO 9000 registration, otherwise the effort will die.

Registration is usually done on a site or facility basis. However, it should not be seen as an isolated effort. Certification should be integrated into the Total Quality Management and strategic effort of the organization. Quality policies and systems in one area should be similar throughout the organization. Of course, quality systems are process- and product-specific, but the intent and the nature of the systems should be transferable across the organization.

No Management Commitment, No Registration

A.G.A. Quality, the registrar of White-Rodgers, will not register a company if management is not committed to the principles of ISO 9000. This is a precondition to registration. Aside from being one of the twenty ISO 9001 elements, management commitment is required for registration maintenance. *A litmus question for many registrars is: Is your company and management committed to quality and purposes of registration?* If the answer is not affirmative, many registrars won't work with companies. Daryl Parker, the manager of A.G.A. Quality, put it this way:

> A.G.A. Quality won't work with and register companies whose management is really not committed to implementing quality systems and integrating them into their operations. It's been our experience that many U.S. companies are not prepared for the ISO registration process. There just doesn't seem to be the right level of management commitment to create the proper quality systems. Companies develop quality systems because they think A.G.A. Quality wants it for registration. Wrong. They should do it because it's good for the company and right for them.

Connect ISO 9000 Registration to Organization's Strategies

Gary Lewis, director of Quality Systems for Amoco Performance Products and member of U.S. Technical 176 advisory committee cautions:

> The need for ISO 9000 registration is often clear-cut, but the path to achieving it isn't. I suggest bridging the gap by developing and documenting the link between the subjective requirements and what is needed to run your business. Start by doing a self-assessment and identify those areas requiring quality system development and improvement. Develop a plan, keeping in mind that the quality strategies must

be tied to the business strategies in order for it to work. Written procedures must be accurate and clearly understood by all. If the procedures are not accurate, they must be changed. "Document what you do, and do what you document."

ESTABLISH A TEAM

Establish a multidisciplinary, interdepartmental, or divisional team to direct and implement the ISO 9000 standard. For example, ISO 9001 addresses the entire product-development cycle from design to installation. The pursuit of registration affects many horizontal organizational areas, processes, and systems. The most effective manner to prepare for registration is through a team.

Who should be on the team? As a general rule, the team should be cross-functional, including quality, manufacturing, purchasing, and engineering professionals. As needs arise, people with area-, process-, or product-specific knowledge and expertise may be asked to join. Once registration is achieved, the team can be disbanded. The purpose of the team is to facilitate the process. Final implementation rests with the operational area. Purchasing is responsible for supplier quality, manufacturing personnel are responsible for production quality, and so on. Operational personnel should be consulted in developing process standards and are responsible for developing procedures and internal quality controls, and ensuring continuous monitoring and continuous process improvement.

ATTEND A CERTIFICATION SEMINAR

If your organization is committed to pursuing registration, then attend a lead assessor or lead auditor seminar. A week-long seminar runs about $1,500–2,000. Attendance and passing a test from an approved course is a prerequisite for becoming a lead assessor. The advantage of the lead assessor seminar is that it shows how quality systems audits are conducted. It can be used to self-assess an operation.

Lead assessor seminars follow the ISO 10011 model of quality auditing and should be approved by the Institute of Quality Assurance (IQA) or the Registration Accreditation Board (RAB).

There are hundreds of ISO 9000 seminars. How does one know which to attend? There is little quality control among seminar presenters. Look for a seminar leader with extensive experience in conducting quality audits.

Develop a Project Schedule, Plan, and Estimate

Seeking registration is not a trivial effort. It requires organizational commitment, resources, and effort. *Most successful efforts follow a project approach.* A project plan and schedule define objectives, leadership, timelines, responsibilities, costs, budget, constraints to be overcome, and resources required. It should be emphasized that the registration is not a minor pursuit. It is costly, not only in terms of direct auditor, consulting, and registration costs but also in terms of opportunity costs.

Hard verifiable estimates of the internal and external costs of ISO certification are difficult to derive. As reported in a recent *Business Week* article, for a manufacturing plant with three hundred employees with an infant quality effort, the registration process can take as long as eighteen months and cost more than $200,000. While the article didn't break down the numbers, it can be assumed that a large part of this cost is the internal costs of pursuing registration.[1]

Retain an ISO 9000 Consultant

> *A consultant is someone who takes your watch away to tell you what time it is.*
> —Ed Finkelstein

If ISO registration is totally new and is being imposed, then consider retaining a consultant. If there is sufficient time to research the process and talk to people, then pursue it on your own.

What can a reputable consultant do? Basically, a consultant can facilitate the registration process. The consultant should be able to assist in the registration and in general inform you how to become registered, how long it should take, how much it will cost, what needs to be done, and who should do it.

Then the consultant should be able to lead you through the registration process. This may simply mean hand holding and answering questions or the consultant may actually lead the effort. It is recommended that if a consultant is retained, then he or she serves in an advisory fashion; that is, to help to guide the effort, evaluate registrars, assess quality documentation, or provide training. ISO registration and its maintenance is ultimately a company's responsibility and should not be abdicated to another party.

[1] "Want EC Business? You Have Two Choices," *Business Week*, October 19, 1992, p. 58.

CONDUCT A PREASSESSMENT

The preassessment, or as it's sometimes called preliminary audit or self-assessment, compares "what is" being done against "what should be" as specified by the quality standard. Compare existing quality documentation and quality systems against the specific ISO 9000 requirements. By this time, a company should know if it must comply with ISO 9001, ISO 9002, or ISO 9003.

The ISO preassessment can be conducted in several ways:

- compare ISO 9000 with what is written

- compare what is written with what is done

- compare the ISO 9000 with what is done

These comparisons should be conducted early in the registration process. Essentially, it is what the quality auditor will actually do. The results of your preassessment indicate how far you should proceed in implementing quality systems and processes that satisfy the specific ISO 9000 requirement. (See the Sample Quality Manual for a set of questions to ask when conducting the preassessment.)

In general, the preassessment informs:

- where the quality systems stand—identifying baselines

- where to go—identifying benchmarks

- how much it will cost—identifying resources

- how much time it will take—identifying timelines

Following the self-assessment, there should be a list of deficiencies and corresponding corrective actions to eliminate each one. Remember, the quality auditor will probably be working off the quality documentation or manual, so these should first be compiled and available. If they aren't, then existing quality documents should be written or upgraded to satisfy the applicable ISO 9000 criteria.

Most quality registrars can conduct a preassessment, audit, and post-audit. The auditee's self-assessment should be conducted before the auditor's preassessment. This provides you the opportunity to evaluate and modify the quality systems without the major expense of a team of auditors at the facility.

Preassessment Benefits

A preassessment will:

- verify the organization is ready for the audit

- increase confidence in passing of the audit

- establish internal baselines from which to measure improvement

- identify resources to pass audit

- identify benchmarks for continuous improvement

- cost less than a formal auditor pre-certification audit

- provide time to make system and process changes

Cycle Approach to Quality Auditing

Another assessment or "look" into the auditing process is to take a step back and identify process cycles or loops such as the product-development process, the production process, the design process, customer complaint–resolution cycle, the problem–corrective action process, and the product life cycle. Follow each cycle from beginning to end and address these questions:

- Are external customer requirements identified?

- Are requirements proceduralized and operationalized?

- Are requirements consistently followed?

- Are there internal controls for monitoring, measuring, controlling, and improving the processes?

- Are internal customers satisfied?

- Are internal processes benchmarked, measured, and improved?

UPGRADE QUALITY DOCUMENTATION

If you have to have a policy manual, publish the ten commandments.
—ROBERT TOWNSEND

Quality systems should be detailed in quality procedures or other quality documents. If a company doesn't have a quality manual or if the manual is window dressing to appease the quality auditor, then a manual should be developed to reflect the applicable ISO 9000 criteria. If quality systems and processes don't follow the manual, then make sure they are aligned with it. Most quality auditors will use the manual to ensure that ISO 9000 quality criteria are addressed.

Some companies think all that's necessary to become registered is to develop a quality manual, have the quality auditor use it as the basis for the audit, and registration is automatic. Unfortunately, this is not so. However, ISO 9000 audits are unique. The auditor does require documentation, whether it's a quality manual or some other quality document. The quality auditor will spend much time verifying and corroborating what is documented is really done. If there is no documentation, an audit can't be conducted. The purpose of the documentation trail is to ensure that customer concerns are defined and communicated internally, and quality systems are developed and operationalized.

Pay Attention to Quality Documentation

The amount and specificity of quality documentation sometimes hinders registration. Some believe that procedures can stifle personal initiative, bureaucratize operations, and waste time. The challenge however is to develop sufficient procedures so that ISO 9000 quality system elements are addressed, and assist, not interfere, with operations.

As well, documentation should be worded carefully. The following caveat is often heard by ISO consultants: "Say what you do and do what you say."

Who Should Develop Procedures?

Quality staff, line personnel, or consultants can develop and write procedures. Interdisciplinary teams from the affected areas may be assigned to work with them.

Be Careful in Writing Quality Documentation

Les Schnoll, Dow Corning ISO Program and Quality Auditing manager, offers this wisdom:

When you document your quality system, you should never *use the words "all" or "never."* As an example, if you state that "all laboratory equipment shall be calibrated," do you really know what you've committed to do? *All* means every piece of glassware, every ruler, every stopwatch must be calibrated.

Calibrating electric timers is fairly simple since AC current is stable, but to calibrate the old hand-held stopwatch, you may have to go back to the atomic clock in Switzerland. If you state that "appropriate laboratory equipment shall be calibrated according to a documented plan," you've said the same thing—but without shooting yourself in both feet. On the other hand, if you state you "never" do something, you will do it on the day of the audit. And, since Murphy is alive and well, the auditor will find it.

Is there a best or optimum way to develop quality procedures? *Internal personnel have the first-hand knowledge to develop procedures that actually reflect what is occurring as opposed to what someone outside the organization thinks is or should be occurring.* Finding available time and overcoming cynical attitudes are major obstacles to be confronted. If work extends into several areas, then an interdisciplinary team may be formed. An outside consultant may also advise the team on the mechanics of writing internal procedures that conform to ISO 9000 specifications.

OVERCOME OBSTACLES AND RESISTANCE

Cynicism, confusion, territoriality/turf, and lack of resources, knowledge, and time are just some of the obstacles that may have to be overcome in your company.

Quality and ISO 9000 cannot be imposed easily. As much as anything, ISO 9000 is an organizational, operational, and procedural change. ISO 9000 technology is relatively easy, but its implementation is more difficult. *People will accept the requirement for self-discipline in direct relation to their personal involvement in the process.* Registration failures can be identified by resistance to change and organizational obstacles. In the quality evolution of the last ten years, people empowerment and involvement are two conventional wisdoms to overcoming these challenges.

KISS Principle of Documentation

Good quality systems documentation is one of the key elements to passing the quality audit. The lead auditor will often work directly off the quality manual or develop a questionnaire based on the manual.

Therefore, follow the KISS Principle in documentation: Keep It Sweet and Simple. The following are tips for developing quality documentation:

- Key the documentation in the manual to the specific ISO 9000 section.

- Do what you say you are doing.

- Develop documentation for what is required in the ISO standard and for ensuring process quality.

- Use standard documentation forms as often as possible.

- Develop levels of documentation in a large facility; for example, at the top there would be a quality policy manual, then quality procedures, work instructions, and so on.

- Use existing procedures as much as possible.

- Write procedures and documentation so they are concise, accurate, complete, understandable, and useful.

ISO 9000 registration is paperwork intensive. Procedures must be developed and followed. To many, this seems like an unnecessary imposition. For companies that have extensive quality systems already in place, this is perceived as redundant.

EVALUATE INTERNAL QUALITY SYSTEMS

Next, evaluate and modify internal quality and operational systems and controls. *By using statistical process control principles, a company can stabilize operations and ensure they are capable of meeting specifications.* By taking this approach, a company will also ensure consistent operations, and quality procedures are kept current and accurate; people are trained; new equipment is purchased; and processes are continuously monitored, measured, and improved.

It's also important to ensure that critical quality processes are in control,

---

This Too Shall Pass

One of the more prevalent obstacles to ISO 9000 registration is employee cynicism. In the last ten years, employees have experienced various quality incarnations, starting from quality circles, statistical process control, employee empowerment, Total Quality Management, and now ISO 9000. People often adopt a "this too shall pass" attitude. It seems there is a new program each year. W. Edwards Deming calls this the "new flavor of the month" program. Employees become cynical that "this program will make their life easier and more productive."

The only way of overcoming employee cynicism is for management to align communications with consistent actions. Cynicism arises when communications and actions diverge.

---

capable, and improving. These last three terms have statistical quality control implications. Essentially, *in control* means that processes are stabilized with no unusual or abnormal process deviation. *Capable* means the process is satisfying customer requirements. *Improving* means: (1) the process is consistently on the specification target, becoming more uniform, and showing less variation; (2) the process is more productive; or (3) the process is producing less deficient products.

If required, modify internal quality systems and controls to increase the likelihood of registration. This may mean modifying internal operations, procedures, controls, systems, and even personnel to ensure uniform quality operations. Remember, the quality audit emphasizes documentation, so ensure documents and control procedures are current, complete, accurate, and doable.

ISO 9000 requires specific systems and procedures are in place, for example:

- internal auditing systems

- documented work instructions

- corrective-action procedures

- training and development procedures

REGISTRATION

Nothing is particularly hard if you divide it into small jobs.
                                —HENRY FORD

The registration stage involves selecting the registrar and working with the auditors. Follow these registration steps:

1. Talk to registrars

2. Select a registrar

3. Complete the registration application

4. Complete the questionnaire

5. Negotiate terms and conditions

6. Plan the audit jointly

7. Schedule the audit

8. Cooperate and coordinate with the auditor

TALK TO REGISTRARS

There are objective and subjective factors in selecting a registrar. The registrar conducts the audit and maintains the register of companies it has audited. In terms of the objective criteria, the following should be considered:

- independence and objectivity

- background of personnel

- experience conducting audits in similar industry

- types of products and processes

- standards used

- financial history

- clients

- registrar status and its certification mark

- list of certified products and manufacturers

- testing and laboratory facilities

- registration queue

Subjective criteria are just as important. They involve how well a company can work with a registrar. Factors to consider are:

- chemistry

- service

- professionalism

- courtesy

- openness

- confidentiality

- fairness

The registrar is offering a product, which is a mixture of the tangible—registration—and the intangible—auditing and advisory services. The registrar can't be hard nosed, failing everyone and not obtaining subsequent business. On the other hand, the registrar can't register unqualified companies without fear of losing its own accreditation. So, most registrars will work with a company knowing that it is mutually beneficial.

The customer must find a registrar with whom he feels relatively comfortable. That registrar will maintain the supplier on a register for many years.

Most Important Questions

Is U.S. registration acceptable in Europe? This has been a critical question for all U.S. registrars. Many U.S. registrars are applying for certification by RAB and by a European accreditor. Currently, some U.S. registrars don't have the joint certification.

Another important question to ask is: What type of EC registration mark does your customer want? Some accreditation marks are more credible than others, such as RvC (the Netherlands), NACCB (UK), and others. These marks dominate because they have established credibility and trust of their audits and certifications. Some marks are not transferable or recognized across national borders. Even in the EC, if you want to sell products in different countries, you may have to secure multiple registration marks.

SELECT A REGISTRAR

As with any purchase decision, the criteria for selecting a registrar should be those that satisfy your quality, performance, cost, delivery, and service requirements. One obvious criterion is the ability to obtain registration. This implies the registrar certifies a high percentage of suppliers. But, a registrar's high "batting average" for first-time registration in the first application may not be in your best interest. One of the biggest problems of selecting registrars involves ethical considerations. Since the U.S. ISO effort is relatively new, it is prone to ethical lapses. Registrars may overpromise and underdeliver, and auditors may be inconsistent in conducting audits or even in interpreting ISO 9000. These problems are understandable when an area is new, so much money is flowing, and the entire process is self-regulated. This situation will hopefully improve in the near future.

Where can you find a list of approved registrars? An approved list may be maintained through the National Institute of Standards and Technology (NIST) or the Registrar Accreditation Board (RAB). (See the Resources section at the back of this book.)

COMPLETE THE REGISTRATION APPLICATION

The registration application is similar for most registrars. The application package will commonly include a cover letter, registrar background information, application form, fee structure, audit requirements, client list, customer questionnaire, and quality documentation request.

COMPLETE THE QUESTIONNAIRE

The purpose of the registrar's questionnaire is to obtain information about your company. The registrar needs to determine if it is capable and qualified to perform the industry- and company-specific audit. Typical questions are:

Nolan's Nuggets of Wisdom

John Nolan, senior quality consultant with UNC Manufacturing Technology, offers the following distilled wisdoms for becoming registered:

1. *ISO 9000 registration provides an internationally recognized mark of excellence.* As a marketing tool, it tears down many barriers.

2. *Let your customer determine the registration marks you attempt to achieve.* Remember, ISO 9000 registration is performed to assure *them*.

3. *Effective internal auditing, management reviews, and corrective action systems separate the great company from the good company.* These quality system elements, perhaps more than any other element, provide the thrust for positive change.

4. *Don't opt for the multiple four-inch binders full of procedures—simple and effective systems can be developed that will leave plenty of room in a one-inch binder.* Many companies develop plans to assure that every detail of the standard is meticulously documented. In doing so, they are laying a mine in the path of long-term implementation and compliance.

5. *The name of the game is not to get registered; the name of the game is to stay registered.*

6. We've done work with firms that have contracted with a registrar that provides a "Preregistration Audit" as part of their "service." The appearance of a conflict of interest in these cases is difficult to ignore. *It's hard to believe that an assessor coming into a facility that has been reviewed by another member of the same organization will not be influenced by that fact.*

7. *The amount of misunderstanding and misinformation provided by some of the "experts" writing in national magazines is astounding.*

8. *For those without a documented quality system, develop such a system—it will be a great help in managing your business.* Record what you *actually do*. Don't waste time on what you think should happen or wish would happen, unless you must in order to meet the standard. Remember, it's your system, and the flexibility of the ISO 9000 standard is what makes it so great.

9. *Prepare early and manage your registration audit.* Remember, the audit team hopes you achieve registration surely as much as you do. Work with the registrar

---

Nolan's Nuggets of Wisdom (*continued*)

---

to develop confidence in your organization's quality vision in every interaction. Be sure all of your manuals are available, and provide any service to make the audit easier.

10. *Training, training, training.* Don't overlook the importance of training. Training can reduce documentation, provide a team-oriented mind-set, and increase morale and efficiency.

- Who are you?

- What products do you produce?

- Where are your plants located?

- How many shifts are there?

- How many employees do you have?

- What is the square footage of your facilities?

- How many sites are there?

- What types of quality certification do you have?

- What types of quality systems and processes do you have?

- Who is in charge of what?

Questionnaire results inform the registrar whether it is capable of conducting an audit and making informed decisions of your quality systems. If you have specialized processes that require specific knowledge, training, and experience, the registrar may decline the assignment and refer you to someone else. Or, the registrar will retain an industry specialist to advise the audit team. Registrars are also accredited to conduct audits and maintain supplier lists in specific industries. If not qualified, then a reputable registrar should notify the customer.

Quality Documentation

The registrar needs to know about your company. Information and documentation should be accurate, complete, understandable, and current. One source is your quality manual. The following documents may also be helpful to the registrar:

- contracts

- purchase orders

- benchmark tests

- quality manuals

- specifications

- engineering prints

- regulatory requirements

- international/national standards

- engineering calculations

- service manuals

- procedures

- policies

- shipping, storage, and packaging information

- workmanship instructions

Negotiate Terms and Conditions

It's important to establish an understanding with the registrar concerning the following issues:

Scope of services. The scope consists of the type of services the customer wants and the registrar can provide. It may include preassessment consulting, auditing, and post-assessment consulting, surveillance auditing, and recertification.

Level of registration. The registrar needs to know the desired level of registration. By the time a company approaches a registrar, it hopefully has followed the recommendations given in the preregistration stage. If not, the registrar can provide EC directives and industry or customer information for a fee.

Consultation. Many registrars provide consulting with their auditing services. Sometimes, this isn't exactly an arms-length transaction. As a result, there can be a problem of real and perceived conflicts of interest.

Time availability. There is currently a queue problem with some registrars. The demand for registrations is higher than the supply of registrars and trained lead auditors. Registrars are overwhelmed by the number of certification requests. So, inquire when the registrar can conduct the audit.

Contract terms. The registrar or the company may have contractual requirements that are unacceptable to the other party. Most registrars object to the consequential damages clause that states the registrar is responsible for damages due to willful or gross negligence. The registrar should explain the registration process so the customer understands what is involved. The registrar will be auditing you every six months, maintaining your name on a register, and every three years conducting a recertification audit. The relationship should be mutually beneficial and trusting.

Confidentiality. When the auditor visits a facility, the auditor or audit team has access to confidential information. The customer should ask the full-time and retained auditors to sign a nondisclosure form.

Use of symbols and logos for advertising or other purposes. Registrars have strict guidelines for using trademarks, logos, and other symbols for advertising. The registrar may own these marks or be a licensee of some accreditation organization. The use of these marks is strictly controlled and regulated.

Costs

The application form has a set fee structure. Presently, the fee structure is not competitive. Demand for registration far exceeds the number of qualified auditors and registrars. As more lead auditors and registrars are qualified then prices will fall and become competitive. Fees can sometimes be negotiated if the work entails multiple sites, consulting, and periodic surveillance. Fees may cover:

- application

- preregistration assessment

- quality documentation assessment

- annual registration

- periodic surveillance

- periodic audit

- corrective action

- follow-up audit

- multiple site audit

- offshore audit

- travel time

- audit recertification

- analysis and reports

- post-audit corrective action analysis

- consulting services

- services (mailing, copying, typing, and faxing)

One item that is sometimes neglected by companies seeking registration is travel costs. It may only cost $X per person per day to audit an offshore facility. Airlines charge a premium for weekday travel, and travel time is also compensated.

Consulting

This is one of the more difficult issues in ISO registration. Traditionally, in operational and financial auditing, the auditor was precluded from supplying consulting services to the area being audited. It presented an appearance of a conflict of interest. I strongly recommend that auditors and consultants come from different organizations.

PLAN THE AUDIT JOINTLY

Preparation is the mark of a professional quality auditor. *Before the audit, the quality auditor should understand your quality systems and processes.* When he or she is at the facility, operations are minimally disrupted. When the auditor or team arrives at the facility, the team has a plan of what to see, where to go, when to do it, how to test it, and when to observe it.

Planning has been coordinated with the customer before the team arrives. The hoped-for result is that false leads are not chased, insignificant items are not tested, and significant items are not overlooked.

As discussed, the registrar will evaluate documentation so it complies with ISO criteria; plan the audit; tailor a questionnaire; and schedule tests and other verification.

SCHEDULE THE AUDIT

The auditor or audit team will visit the company's operations and evaluate quality systems. This can disrupt operations. *It's essential that the lead auditor and the customer jointly organize and schedule the audit.* Work with the auditor to determine his or her requirements.

Issues to address are:

- providing all quality documentation

- arranging space, resources, tools, equipment, and facilities the audit team may require

- identifying escort

- arranging meetings and other requirements

- notifying employees of audit

COOPERATE AND COORDINATE WITH THE AUDITOR

During the audit, the auditor or audit team will gather and evaluate data so there is sufficient information for them to arrive at an audit opinion of conformance to the applicable ISO 9000 quality system requirements. Quality systems are compared against quality policies and standards. Quality processes are compared

---

Educate, Don't Indoctrinate

One company pursuing registration tried to educate all its employees on what to say, how to say it, and when to say it when the auditors visited. For example, the company told employees not to talk with the auditor unless spoken to. The company did not want the employees to volunteer information that would lead to a corrective action, adverse audit opinion, loss of proprietary data, or loss of existing customers.

The company needed the registration as a condition of business from some customers so it was somewhat paranoid. Unfortunately, employee education was perceived as a euphemism for indoctrination. The relationship between the auditor and the company degenerated and became adversarial. The company still passed and secured registration. The question arises: How well will employees follow the new quality procedures and maintain quality systems that will be reevaluated during surveillance and its recertification? The registration process was painful to all parties and did not instill or reinforce an organizational quality ethic.

---

against procedures, process charts, and work descriptions. Work is compared against instructions.

What will the auditor do if there is no or insufficient quality documentation? During the preassessment the auditor will notify the customer to proceed no further until documentation exists and quality systems are implemented.

The auditor or company team can conduct the audit in several ways. The important point is that the auditors feel secure ISO 9001/9002/9003 requirements are addressed and properly implemented. Auditors will seek assurance through observing operations, interviewing personnel, evaluating risks, evaluating internal control structure, testing the effectiveness of the internal control structure, evaluating audit evidence, and issuing an opinion.[2]

POSTREGISTRATION

At the conclusion of the audit, complete the following:

1. Schedule a meeting with the auditor
2. Correct deficiencies

[2] G. Hutchins, *Quality Auditing* (Englewood Cliffs, NJ: Prentice Hall, 1992), p. 103.

3. Pursue continuous improvement

4. Maintain registration

5. Anticipate surveillance visits

6. Apply for recertification

SCHEDULE A MEETING WITH THE AUDITOR

During or after the audit, meet with the auditor or team. *If the audit is intensive or extensive, daily progress meetings can be arranged.* If the audit has a limited scope, arrange for a meeting with the auditor at the end of the audit. Periodic meetings reduce the possibility of surprises or major unresolved differences.

The audit report communicates the auditor's findings and opinions derived from the audit. The report communicates the state of conformance of the existing quality systems to ISO 9001/9002/9003 requirements, which will result in registration. Or the report will communicate Corrective Action Requests (CARs). Upon implementation of the CARs, certification will be completed.

Most audit reports follow a consistent format, usually including the following sections: executive summary, introduction, findings, Corrective Action Requests, and background tests and information.

CORRECT DEFICIENCIES

The auditor may detect deficiencies, also called *nonconformances.* Some may be minor and others major. The auditor will issue a Corrective Action Request for those the auditor believes are critical, major, or recurring. Is a CAR issued for all deficiencies? Usually not, only if the nonconformance relates directly to ISO 9000 criteria. In surveillance or recertification, a CAR may be issued for:

- noncompliance with ISO requirement

- weak or no internal controls

- health, welfare, or environmental deterioration

- recurring problems

- high-risk conditions

Is it up to the auditor to specify how the correction will be conducted? No. Some auditors may specify in general terms what has to be done to fix and correct the problem. *However, this is not the function of the auditor in a compliance audit. The auditor should note the area and the deficiency and then rely on the auditee to determine the "fix."* The fix eliminates the symptom and the correction eliminates the root cause.

Following successful corrective action, a certificate of registration is issued and the company's name goes on a register of certified companies. Each registrar has rules and regulations about its marks and logos that must be followed. These often restrict their use. Most U.S. registrars, for example, follow the European model in which the mark can't be placed on the product to imply or denote "quality."

PURSUE CONTINUOUS IMPROVEMENT

ISO registration is often just a step in the continuous improvement process. The customer may require more comprehensive ISO 9000 registration or even establish higher levels of certification. The higher levels may be ISO 9004, a European quality award, Malcolm Baldrige, or other criteria.

MAINTAIN REGISTRATION

Once achieved, registration cannot be dismissed. *It requires day-to-day attention to quality processes and operations.*

The maintenance of the conformity certificate requires:

- maintaining and controlling quality documentation and specifically the quality manual in compliance to the specific ISO 9000 standard

- notifying the registrar of major quality system changes

- developing and maintaining an approved supplier procedure or similar documentation

- providing access to the registrar's auditors

- appointing a management representative to be responsible for all certification requirements

- using the registrar's marks and symbols only as permitted

ANTICIPATE SURVEILLANCE VISITS

Registration maintenance requires six-month surveillance visits. They can be scheduled or unscheduled. Scheduled audits are announced and planned in accordance with the certificate of conformity.

Unscheduled surveillance is an unannounced visit to verify that quality systems are in place and working properly. These are usually conducted as a result of a complaint, major publicity, litigation, product failure, or some other major incident. A registrar may also conduct an unscheduled audit if the certificate holder does not inform the registrar of major operational or quality systems changes.

Certificate Suspension and Cancellation

A registrar can suspend certificates of conformance based on certain conditions, including:

- fraud, negligence, or other actions that may impugn the registrar's reputation

- requested corrective actions not being completed by the timeline

- marks or symbols being used improperly

- the company not informing the registrar of changes to the certified quality system.

As a last resort, a registration can also be canceled. The registrar exercises this option carefully. A certificate may be canceled if the certificate holder:

- does not correct major symptom and root-cause nonconformances

- does not correct the conditions that led to the suspension

- does not pay fees

- acts in a fraudulent or highly negligent manner

The above alternatives can be appealed to the registrar's management or higher accreditation bodies. *The registrar will seldom go through this process because a registrar perceived as unfair may have problems capturing business.*

Apply for Recertification

There are still inconsistencies among certification and testing bodies. One question is: How often should a company be completely recertified—every three, four, or more years? There are international requirements for periodic or surveillance audits to ensure that the quality systems are operating properly. However, *there is no international requirement for a complete recertification audit.*

Private accreditors and registrars see recertification audits as a necessary requirement of ongoing and improving quality. The rationale often heard is that an organization is a living mechanism of management, goal, plan, system, and process changes. Each change is a source of additional variation that may enhance or degrade quality. Complete recertification audits would catch and presumably prevent quality system deterioration. On the other hand, I've heard the rejoinder from registered companies that recertification audits are a guaranteed source of income for registrars.

In most cases, the contractual boilerplate of most registrars stipulates recertification every three years. The registrar will completely reaudit the customer's facilities. By this time, the registrar has accumulated information from the initial audit and subsequent surveillance visits.

The registrar knows the company well and has the following on file:

- audit plans

- interview results

- preassessments

- quality documentation and manuals

- engineering prints

- audit reports

- Corrective Action Requests

- calculations

- deficiency findings

- process flowcharts

WHY DO WE NEED TO DO ISO 9000?

"Why do we need to be certified and registered to ISO 9000? We already have a TQM program that is much further advanced than ISO 9000. This is a waste of time."

A company will probably hear this and more in the registration effort. To be successful, almost everyone—from senior management to the line person—has to understand and be convinced of its value. It takes time and patience. But the rewards are large. Without understanding and cooperation, people may hinder the registration effort, fail to take ownership, or not support it at all. If employees won't take ownership, then ISO 9000 will be perceived as another "here today and gone tomorrow" management imposition. So, work slowly and steadily to ensure the relevance of ISO 9000 is understood by all.

CHAPTER 9

Successful Registration:
The White-Rodgers Story

There is no finish line.
—NIKE CORPORATION MOTTO

When leading ISO experts were asked to identify who's got a world-class ISO operation, one company was frequently mentioned—White-Rodgers (W-R), a division of Emerson Electric. White-Rodgers is an ISO 9000 success model for your company to follow.

There are several other reasons why White-Rodgers was chosen:

- It was one of the first companies in the U.S. to become registered to ISO 9001.

- The natural-gas appliance industry was one of the first sectors targeted by an EC directive for conformity assessment to essential requirements.

- It was the first company in the natural-gas industry sector to become registered in the U.S. Its registration number is 001 from A.G.A. Quality, the registrar.

- ISO 9000 was used as an external and internal model—externally to become competitive and to satisfy customers, and internally as a means to improve operations.

This model is illustrative of how registration is achieved and, more important, how it is used to stay competitive. From talking to many companies and auditors, the experiences of W-R are common to many companies seeking registration.

White-Rodgers Executive Commitment

White-Rodgers (W-R) has the following fundamental guiding principles, which dovetail nicely into the ISO registration effort:

1. *To develop a highly skilled work force at all levels of the organization.* Routine training will occur in statistical process control (SPC), job requirements, and company operation expectations.

2. *That the key principle of manufacturing will be to minimize the variation of parts and products* from each machine and operation throughout production.

3. *Quality and customer satisfaction is dependent upon consistency.* Therefore, to assure consistency and *routine* satisfaction of customers, White-Rodgers will have a system of product and process documentation. Product specifications will detail every aspect of product performance in consistent language. Processes will be defined through manufacturing specifications by showing enough detail for anyone to do the job and also by conveying the specific quality requirements at that operation.

4. *Customer satisfaction with new products on initial shipments* is critical to obtaining future business. As we introduce new products or processes, product requirements, process specifications, and quality requirements will be released on or before the first production run.

5. *Continuous effort to assure system reliability will occur.* Therefore, new product development will always include an internal product FMEA (Failure Mode Effects Analysis) where applicable. An external FMEA will also be performed on safety-related products and features.

6. *Major new processes or revisions to processes will require an internal process FMEA prior to production release.*

(continued on the following page)

White-Rodgers Executive Commitment (*continued*)

7. *New processes or machines will require a statistical capability study prior to acceptance for production.*

8. *Suppliers are partners in the success of White-Rodgers.* As a primary objective, we must provide adequate part specifications. W-R's selection of a supplier is based on total performance (not price alone) and a formal approval system, involving Purchasing, Engineering, and Quality Assurance.

9. *Productivity improves as quality improves.* Consequently, accountability measurements of scrap and other PONC (Price of Nonconformance) are utilized with all employees.

10. *A roadblock to quality improvement is continuous acceptance of what has always been.* Performance expectations will be specifically built around the unacceptability of routine inconsistent reject rates. Also, it is expected that procedures will be followed as part of the performance expectation to achieve consistency.

11. *Quality system audits will be periodically performed.* Audit teams will monitor procedure compliance, product and process conformance as well as availability of requirements to the user of documentation.

12. *Product approval for a new product release requires the formal signed release by Production, Engineering, Marketing, and Quality Assurance.*

13. *Our goal is to have continual improvement in quality.* W-R has an excellent reputation for quality, and we are committed to continuing that position. In this respect, the customer is always our focal point.

GETTING STARTED

It is a funny thing about life, if you refuse to accept anything but the best, you very often get it.
—SOMERSET MAUGHAM

Who is White-Rodgers? White-Rodgers, headquartered in St. Louis, is an autonomous division of Emerson Electric. It is primarily nonunion and has approximately thirty-four hundred employees.

The company provides critical products to the natural-gas industry, including gas ignition systems, thermostats, burners, hot water controls, and gas regulators. The EC developed a directive that specifically requires conformity assessment of these products.

WHO ARE THE PLAYERS?

> *Leadership is the capacity to translate vision into reality.*
> —WARREN BENNIS, Educator

Major organizational changes require people to assume different roles. At W-R, the principals in the registration efforts were John Cichy, President, who introduced the concept and provided the initial impetus; Bill Cromer, Director of Quality, who provided the overall guidance across functional and organizational lines; and Norm Siefert, Director of Quality Services, who was the initial champion and later the technical day-to-day manager of the registration effort.

WHAT CAUSED OR DROVE THE REGISTRATION EFFORT?

Different forces were converging on U.S. business in the early 1980s. Peters and Waterman had just written *In Search of Excellence*. A national quality ethic was emerging. New business wisdoms were becoming widely accepted and adopted, such as quality control, zero defects, prevention, customer focus, and worker empowerment.

Many companies were asking: Are we doing the "right" things right? Similarly, W-R was pursuing this self-inquiry. It had a high-product quality reputation. But could things be done better, both in terms of making the product better and in terms of satisfying the external customer? Customer expectations were rising and W-R's internal quality costs were high. It also recognized that its product lines had to be one hundred percent conforming to customer requirements.

W-R's excellent quality reputation was reactive, however. A customer once told a W-R manager: "If there's a problem with a W-R product, we know that we will always get quick action." Inspection was used throughout its operations. However, inspection did not catch mistakes at the source and prevent future deficiencies. W-R wanted to move quality further upstream and change its focus to prevention. While external customer satisfaction was high, internal quality costs were commensurately high. This reflected the high costs of inspection and testing. It considered adopting new operating concepts and a philosophy based on modern quality control and assurance concepts.

SEEKING A COMMON LANGUAGE OF QUALITY

By late 1985, White-Rodgers was ready for a division-wide change, a change to a prevention culture. The focus was primarily on product quality. Everyone was included.

But first, W-R realized it needed a common language in quality that everyone could understand and use to communicate. *Not developing a common language is a cardinal mistake of many firms when they try to modify a business culture, direction, or objective.* Management becomes indoctrinated in new business paradigms and language. However, sometimes the new language is not translated and transferred to all employees. And once management has pontificated its message, six months elapse and management wonders why nothing has been accomplished. The problem is the average employee sees the "new thought" or "new speak" as another imposition or indoctrination. And this breeds doubt, resistance, and hostility.

W-R recognized this phenomenon and wanted to establish a common foundation language. After evaluating alternatives, Phil Crosby's quality language and methodology was seen as the best W-R fit. All division management, from the president to plant managerial staff, attended Crosby's quality college over a two-and-a-half-year period. Crosby tapes were purchased. As one person said: "Training was White-Rodgerized," meaning customized to W-R's requirements and needs. "Train the trainer" was then instituted at all facilities to transfer the quality training and inculcate a common language. The original training nucleus was in team building and communications. This laid the foundation for the soft side of quality, specifically in terms of developing a common language, direction, skills, ethos, and objectives.

TYING THE SOFT SIDE WITH THE HARD SIDE

Simultaneously, W-R focused on implementing quality education into specific problem solving and process control on the production line. There were also courses in statistical process control (SPC), quality planning, and design of experiments. These areas are considered technical, the hard side of quality.

However, two separate paths were evolving, the soft side and the hard side.

Natural Gas Appliance Directive

White-Rodgers sells products in the EC so it must comply with the Natural Gas Appliance Directive. The Natural Gas Appliance Directive states the essential safety requirements as well as the means (the modules) by which suppliers can comply. The directive and the modules are discussed in Chapter 5.

A supplier of natural-gas appliances and equipment can certify conformity through Module B: EC Type Examination—a notified or approved body checks and certifies that a gas appliance, representative of production, meets the directive's provisions.

As mentioned in Chapter 5, this module is usually used in conjunction with another module. In the case with gas appliances, the manufacturer can opt for one of the following:

- Module C: Conformity to Type

- Module D: Production Quality Assurance (ISO 9002 compliance)

- Module E: Product Quality Assurance (ISO 9003 compliance)

- Module F: Product Verification

W-R searched for a system that was going to bridge and tie both quality approaches to a common structure. W-R wanted something to operationalize quality into the organization. Existing documentation could not express or describe the new quality direction. They were looking for a quality umbrella.

BS 5750

In 1985, John Cichy, the president of W-R, had been visiting one of W-R's major UK customers, which had just gone through BS 5750 registration, the predecessor to ISO 9000. The customer extolled the benefits of registration and recommended it to Cichy. BS 5750 presented an excellent introductory quality-system structure. W-R recognized that its quality initiatives were going to evolve and progress well beyond it. As well, it served as the driver to other things that had to be done. Documentation systems had to be tightened up. The soft and hard sides of quality had to be integrated.

UK CONSULTANTS

W-R initially worked with the UK-based consultants that had advised W-R's customer on registration. Consultants interviewed people at three plants and developed procedures. The consultants described the scope of the standard, wrote policies and procedures based on what was being done, and constructed W-R's quality systems manual. Internal resources were dedicated to achieve the aggressive schedule that was established to become registered.

ISO 9000

While W-R pursued certification to BS 5750, ISO 9000 was released in 1987. ISO 9000 was similar to BS 5750 and was at that time already seen as potentially becoming a global quality standard. *ISO 9000 was not a Total Quality Management (TQM) package, but more of a ground-floor quality system in terms of addressing many quality systems requirements.* ISO 9000 formed a common linkage between the soft side and hard side of quality by pulling together quality documentation, training responsibility, management auditing, and other quality system requirements.

The original driver in pursuing BS 5750 certification was the integration of diverse quality efforts into a mechanism that would allow continuous improvement. While BS 5750 did not emphasize process improvement, it proved an excellent vehicle to start the quality journey and be a foundation to define W-R's basic quality requirements.

An important element of Crosby's approach is "Do it right the first time." One of the early challenges to W-R was to define the "its" to do right the first time. One advantage of ISO 9001 was that it generically covered twenty quality system elements, and the standard helped define the "its" in terms of generic quality systems requirements.

HOW IT WAS MANAGED

Norm Siefert chaired the ISO 9001 registration project. He pursued it as a project specifying timelines, accountabilities, budgets, and resources. Project teams were established for implementing Crosby's ideas and for complying with each separate systems requirement. Area teams defined needs and worked with consultants to develop procedures. Registration of three plants took two and a half years. Operational responsibility for registration rested with the plant quality managers.

AMERICAN GAS ASSOCIATION LABORATORIES

In 1987, the American Gas Association Laboratories became active with quality systems registration within the gas industry. The American Gas Association Quality is a gas industry trade association laboratory that tests and certifies gas products such as gas appliances, furnaces, and components. Once approved, they carry an A.G.A.L. seal of approval.

At the time, A.G.A. Laboratories was aware of the European Gas Appliance Directive, which allowed different conformity assessment options. A.G.A. Laboratories had traditionally been product-oriented, meaning they had been testing products to industry and U.S. government requirements. A.G.A.L. adopted ISO 9000 as a means of monitoring quality systems and complying with the European directive, and thereafter became a registrar. A.G.A.L. expanded its thinking from product to system/process as it recognized the advantages of changing from inspection to prevention. A.G.A.L. realized that in the evolution of quality it had to take the industry lead to promote prevention and a quality system orientation.

Who Is A.G.A. Quality?

A.G.A. Laboratories, White-Rodgers's registrar, was the first U.S. certification agency to offer and market quality systems registration. A.G.A. Laboratories has followed an evolutionary path similar to other certification bodies that started offering ISO systems registration in addition to product testing.

A.G.A. Laboratories was founded in 1925 for the primary purpose of testing natural-gas appliances. As the principal U.S. approvals agency for equipment used in the residential and commercial gas products, A.G.A. engineers evaluated appliance product plans and conducted in-plant production inspections. Presently more than five hundred manufacturers participate in the A.G.A. certification program in which approved products bear A.G.A.'s certification label, a star symbol.

Anticipating more of a preventive, systems orientation to certification, A.G.A. Quality was formed as a division of A.G.A. Laboratories to conduct third-party ISO 9000 auditing and registration. Continuing to build domestic and international mutual recognition linkages, A.G.A. Quality has Memoranda of Understanding (MOU) for quality system registration with counterparts in France, Canada, Germany, and the Netherlands.

Source: A.G.A. Quality Publication, 1992.

HOW WAS THE REGISTRAR CHOSEN?

W-R's product lines, previous liaison in product testing, and other factors formed the basis for the registration relationship. A.G.A.L. was the first registrar, and W-R was the first registered company in the gas industry. It was a natural fit, A.G.A. Quality already had tested and certified W-R's products.

Three plants, Affton, Batesville, and Harrison, were initially registered to ISO 9001 in 1989. The registration has been maintained through six-month surveillance visits, which continue to certify W-R's quality systems. W-R's goal is to have five plants registered to ISO 9001 by 1995. The purpose of having other plants certified is to communicate continuing quality commitment to customers.

Maintenance of the certification is almost as important as achieving the registration. Registration is maintained through announced six-month surveillance audits. During these visits, A.G.A. Quality auditors visit the plant and check about one quarter of the quality system requirements. Two elements almost always checked are internal auditing and corrective action because they involve all the system elements. If there is a minor deficiency, the auditor will review the deficiency in the following audit. If there is a major deficiency or a major quality system change, the auditor will recommend a reaudit in thirty days. There haven't been any major deficiencies up to this date.

INITIAL CONSTRAINTS

An initial obstacle to the primary ISO registration effort was time requirements in developing ISO specific documentation. This often meant creating documents from scratch.

Another constraint was that people were skeptical about registration. A part of the initial resistance was the feeling there was something else to do on top of everything else. Change is difficult. W-R employees asked some tough questions: "What does this do for us?" "Is it worth it?" "This is a lot of work to go through, so what?" "Are we really going to follow these procedures once they're written?"

In retrospect, several people remarked that ISO 9000 worked because it had top-management support and the approach was evolutionary, not revolutionary. Major organizational changes did not have to be imposed on W-R. W-R already had good quality systems in place and operating successfully. And, most importantly, customers were reasonably satisfied.

THE PRESENT SITUATION

ISO 9000 has almost become routine. Everyone understands the purpose of the surveillance audits. New employees are trained in ISO 9000. Quality systems are regularly monitored. Measurements indicate company-wide improvement. According to internal surveys, employees are satisfied.

However, by 1989 quality improvements had slowed. The easy improvements had been made, and now the hard work had to start—digging into the company to understand underlying operations, identifying systemic sources of variation, and eliminating chronic problems.

In 1990, W-R realized that plateaus of quality had been reached and momentum was at a standstill. So believing in Crosby's 14th step ". . . Do it all over again," W-R relaunched a quality improvement initiative. New quality improvement teams were created, especially at office headquarters. Initial efforts had been product-oriented on the shop floor and the office environment had been neglected.

The revitalization worked in 1990 and 1991. A lot of people were won over again. The emphasis was on empowerment and quality improvement. Employees were asked what they could do for themselves to improve their work area. This resonated with them because they were being asked what *they* could do to improve *their* quality of work life. According to Norm Siefert, "The communication and self-satisfaction that came out of that effort is immeasurable. *Because people saw they could have an effect on what they were doing on a daily basis.* People talked with each other to figure out what could be done better, which was extremely important to the people who have to do it every day. Now, they are believers. They do have control."

The other lesson from W-R is that the quality journey never stops. New goals have been established, specifically to have all plants ISO 9001 registrable and to lower the cost of quality by 6 percent per year, which will drive quality improvement, lower parts per million (PPM) nonconformance levels on key products, and achieve 95 percent on-time shipments to customers.

QUALITY DOCUMENTATION

Put the policy manual back on the shelf when common sense points to a better way.

—THOMAS BONOMA

In 1985 BS 5750 requirements caused W-R's entire documentation system to be redesigned and reborn at all levels, including policy, procedures, and workmanship documentation. W-R discovered that accepted documentation is the foundation of the ISO 9000 quality initiative.

As much as possible, W-R integrated ISO 9000 requirements with its preexisting quality documentation program. *To W-R, quality documentation is a living document.* It evolves to reflect changing needs and requirements. *ISO requirements are also W-R business requirements and vice versa.* W-R, in a generic sense, realized that they were a good way to conduct business.

Quality documentation was a vehicle to define requirements and a structure to train people to the requirements. "The basic foundation of quality was to define requirements, train people, provide them with resources, and wait to get consistent results," according to Siefert.

LESSONS LEARNED FROM WRITING PROCEDURES

An important lesson learned by W-R was to write procedures that reflect how things are actually done. If an external contractor is writing the procedures, that person must thoroughly understand operations. A problem may occur if this person does not understand or notice some operational nuance and develops incorrect procedures.

There are several warning signs about procedures. It's possible that someone who should have read a procedure did not and is doing her or his "own thing." Sometimes it becomes a matter of determining whether the procedure should be changed or if the employee's methods should be changed.

Another warning sign is to develop a quality system that doesn't become too proceduralized so that product quality does not improve. Clearly, a person can follow all the procedures and not have product quality or a satisfied customer.

When developing policy and procedures, don't make them a wish list. They should be reasonable and reflect what can be done. Procedures should be written to current operating guidelines.

Once procedures are drafted and approved, the difficult work then begins. The easy part is writing the procedures; the hard part is ensuring they are followed day after day. "It is easy to develop procedures and relatively easy to initially implement them, but more difficult to carry them out day to day once the initial excitement wears off," said Barry Wilfong, a plant quality manager.

HIERARCHY OF QUALITY MANUAL

W-R developed its quality manual in a hierarchical fashion, with the highest level consisting of policies and procedures. The manual is designed to be traceable, by paragraph number, to ISO 9001 paragraph and section numbers to all twenty elements as a practical matter to facilitate the conduct of the audit. W-R also added two additional sections—quality measurement and customer satisfaction.

Operational documents at first were also placed in the quality manual. The three-level hierarchy became unwieldy and not user-friendly. The operating manual incorporated material that was not directly addressed or aligned to ISO 9001. The registrar had problems following the audit trail. The manual was subsequently reorganized to include two levels of documentation.

Level 1, the highest level of the manual, deals with policy and applies to the entire W-R division and its eight plants. It is generic and addresses all ISO 9001 twenty elements, including customer satisfaction and quality measurement. It also includes specific procedures that apply to the entire division.

Level 2 consists of plant-specific procedures that address the twenty ISO 9001 elements. All plants are not identical. Each plant has different products, processes, and structure. They aren't mirror images of each other.

A valuable feature of the W-R quality manual is that all quality systems are closed-loop networks. For example, a corrective action closed loop ensures that problems are identified and corrected and don't recur.

HAS IT BEEN WORTH IT?

W-R was years ahead of the marketplace in adopting ISO 9000 and its predecessor, BS 5750. The decision to adopt it was not market- or EC-directive driven. ISO 9000 was initially seen as a quality improvement tool for running the business, based on customer satisfaction through quality.

Redefining Taylor: The NUMMI Experience

In a recent *Harvard Business Review* article, Paul Adler asserts that procedural standardization can benefit a "learning" organization. His research based on NUMMI, a GM-Toyota joint venture, offers significant insights into the application of ISO 9000 standards.

Frederick Winslow Taylor, the father of time and motion studies, asserted that standards and discipline are the foundation of productivity and profits. He postulated that:

1. Efficiency and quality in routine and repetitive activities is assured through standardized work procedures.

2. Standardization diminishes incentives, energy, and creativity.

3. Results are poor quality, low interest, strikes, and high absenteeism.

4. The solution: More authoritarian control over recalcitrant employees.

Adler's insight is that the second premise is false. Formal work standards developed by industrial engineers or by those perceived as outsiders are "alienating." However, "procedures that are designed by the workers themselves in a continuous, successful effort to improve productivity, quality, skills, and understanding can humanize even the most disciplined forms of bureaucracy." Adler offers NUMMI as an example of the new "learning bureaucracy."

Standards developed by those who have to use and live with them day by day can be an empowerment mechanism. Standards developed by teams of workers are perceived as a form of self-control, not as something imposed from above or from outside the workplace.

Adler's insights are counter-intuitive. Contemporary psychological and humanist wisdom maintains that Taylor's machinelike interpretation of human behavior and standardization are anachronistic.

Does it work? As a GM plant, one manager referred to it as "the worst plant in the world." As GM-Toyota, absenteeism dropped from 20–25 percent during the GM days to 3–4 percent now; participation in the suggestion system is close to 92 percent; its "lean" production methods are a national showcase of productivity and quality improvement.

Source: P. Adler, "Time-and-Motion Regained," *Harvard Business Review*, January–February 1993, pp. 97–107.

The bottom-line question I asked many W-R employees was: "Has ISO registration been worth it?" The following represent some of the comments I received. "To W-R, all quality improvement is an investment, and it's been the best investment in quality that we've got," according to Bill Cromer, W-R's director of quality. *"In terms of definable and measurable cost of quality, the payoff was in its ability to be more competitive,"* according to another manager. The following are comments from a number of managers and employees about ISO registration:

- Improves competitive advantage

- Proceduralizes operations

- Makes operations consistent

- Builds customer relationships

- Helps establish a "quality" company

- Encourages self-assessment

- Empowers employees

- Establishes internal trust

- Improves communications

IMPROVES COMPETITIVE ADVANTAGE

When W-R started using BS 5750, there was little competitive advantage to registration. No one knew about it except some people in the United Kingdom. There it was used as an accepted guideline to building a proper quality system. Bill Cromer said: "Today we recognize the competitive advantage of being certified as our customers are coming to us and asking, 'Will you help and tell us about it.'"

Quality is considered a part of the competitive global benchmarking process at W-R. Siefert added: *"A substantial portion of our business gains in recent years has been attributable to quality, and a substantial part of the losses of our competitor's business to us has been due to quality.* If our quality was the same as it was three years ago, we would have a problem."

Who Should Be Your Registrar?

A question that often comes up is: Who is your registrar? For W-R, A.G.A. Quality was a natural choice. However, many companies spend an inordinate amount of time searching for the "right" registrar. Bill Cromer has some interesting advice:

> Many companies that want certification spend a lot of time worrying about who is going to certify them. They think that if they get the wrong one, then all this is wasted. That isn't the case. The issue is to have the internal systems and controls so that one can pass anybody's audit and certification. If you've got the quality systems in place, it follows that you should be able to pass. First, get started on the work, then worry about who is going to certify you. If a registrar doesn't do what it is supposed to do for you in the EC or elsewhere, pick another one. It may be another expense, but not the much higher expense to get organized to be certified.

PROCEDURALIZES OPERATIONS

The process of pursuing registration facilitates proceduralizing operations. One reason often offered for Japanese competitiveness is that it is a country with a common culture and homogeneous population. In this often-used stereotype, the Japanese think detail, are very precise, and are always conscious of quality. Experts maintain this is a cultural ethic. While it may be so, another factor often neglected or dismissed is the Japanese focus on proceduralizing even the smallest series of actions.

Why can't we copy this behavior? Pundits speculate we can't because we haven't been enculturated to these expectations. Wrong! Proceduralizing is critical in many regulated industries, such as nuclear power, aerospace, pilot training, and power system. If the will is there, it is possible in any country.

"Americans are real serious about procedures when life and death is at stake. Some say Americans shoot from the hip or fly by the seat of our pants. These are excuses Americans make when not wanting to think through the things they are doing and stick to them and be ready to change them, if necessary," according to Cromer.

Procedures got a bad reputation because they were seen as unchangeable. At White-Rodgers, they're on a slip of paper, not chiseled in stone. Again, according to Cromer, "They're there until someone has a better idea, and people agree the procedures should be changed."

MAKES OPERATIONS CONSISTENT

> *Management by objective works if you know the objectives. Ninety percent of the time you don't.*
> —PETER DRUCKER

A major benefit of proceduralizing operations was to make W-R's operations more consistent and uniform. In terms of operations, lack of consistency is the root cause of unwanted variation. Unwanted variation is the source of nonconformances or poor quality.

Important elements of Crosby's training involve identifying requirements, training people, dedicating resources, and auditing internal operations. As Siefert says: *"Part of W-R's culture and training is that consistency is the root cause of quality.* No matter if you're in the shop environment making hard products or whether you're in data processing or a secretary, it's consistency. Once you've got your requirements established, you try to meet them all the time."

Consistency, uniformity, and lack of variation are all emphasized in ISO documentation. *This principle is extended to all operations and is considered a basic W-R management principle.*

BUILDS CUSTOMER RELATIONSHIPS

ISO registration builds good customer relationships. It also helps when there are problems by letting the customer know that the supplier is committed to quality and has a registered quality system.

W-R used ISO registration to open customers' doors. Most W-R customers are aware of the registration. In many cases, White-Rodgers was instrumental in making its customers aware and interested in it. In some cases, registration has allowed White-Rodgers to skip steps in its customers' supplier-certification hurdles.

In many cases, medium-sized W-R customers accept ISO 9001 registration in lieu of their own quality certification. Major customers may still insist on compliance to their process-specific quality-certification requirements to be on their approved supplier lists. Or these large customers will accept ISO 9001 registration contingent on defect-free product shipments over a specific period of time.

HELPS ESTABLISH A "QUALITY" COMPANY

At W-R, ISO 9000 is part of a total quality effort of satisfying customers and improving continuously. ISO registration is not a stand-alone operation.

Cromer commenting on this emphasized:

> ISO by itself does not make a company a quality company. If a company does not have the intent of having a quality culture or a company-wide quality improvement process, then they will have a terrible time with ISO 9000. It won't fit anywhere. It will drive a company to do a bunch of things that won't make sense and will cause inconsistencies in the company's communications to its people. The conflicts are going to be horrendous.

ENCOURAGES SELF-ASSESSMENT

ISO implementation forced W-R to investigate what was being done and how it was being done. *This self-assessment encouraged people to address their personal and independent agendas as they were encouraged to talk with one another during the registration process.* ISO 9000 requirements are not stand-alone. They require interdepartmental cooperation and coordination. "A lot of people are now talking to one another that did not talk to each other before," reported one employee.

EMPOWERS EMPLOYEES

> *Looking for differences between more productive and less productive organizations we found that the most striking difference is the number of people who are involved and feel responsibility for solving problems.*
> —MICHAEL MCTAGUE, Management
> Consultant

ISO 9000 documentation and training ensure everyone knows his or her job. At W-R, quality cost data are shared with people on the plant floor. People are empowered. If anything unusual occurs on the line, employees can stop the production process. Problems are resolved at the level at which they occur. Problems are brought up the supervisory chain when resources must be dedicated or an issue requires higher resolution. Line supervision evolves into process facilitators and guides and it allows supervision to manage by exception.

As well, employees are accountable. Production and quality reports are shared with employees. Scrap and rework of direct labor data are shared with everyone.

Tactical Benefits of Registration

Siefert saw the following ISO 9000 benefits from a day-to-day operational perspective:

1. Provided a very good base for understanding quality. It became part of the common divisional language of quality and the way things are done.
2. Minimized and in some cases eliminated interdepartmental finger pointing and separation of agendas. This aided horizontal communication.
3. Improved the consistency of the way things are done.
4. Helped to define internal requirements and in general improved internal communications.
5. Communicated management's quality expectations to the organization. It brought top management's concerns closer to the worker.
6. Helped with marketshare, visibility, credibility, and opened customer doors. We had the first registered sites in our industry in the U.S.
7. Contributed to profitability, directly to the bottom line.

ESTABLISHES INTERNAL TRUST

The key to quality success is to ensure that everyone works together—loyalty up the organization leads to loyalty down the organization. It is management's responsibility to ensure that employees have the right tools and are empowered to parcel out work area responsibilities.

Roger Gross, a W-R plant manager, said: "There has to be the trust that I'll keep up my end of the bargain if you'll keep up yours. Give them—the employees—the proper tools, and they will build a quality product. The hourly people will point things out to you. Instead of having problems occur for days on end, we stop the process and fix the problems. This is just smart management."

IMPROVES COMMUNICATIONS

A person has been doing a job for twenty-five years, and management is going to tell the person how to do it. And someone imposes his or her interpretation through a procedure of how it should be done. This usually evokes a sullen or resistant response.

According to Gross, "It's amazing the amount of work that is done based on history that no one can account for as well as using drawings that have been superseded or modified. ISO documentation sets up a common language and ensures understanding across engineering, manufacturing, and the shop floor."

Given Hindsight

Given hindsight, I asked Siefert: "What would you have done differently?" He detailed the following:

1. Write all the quality procedures ourselves, instead of relying on consultants.

2. Have more of an interdepartmental effort developing the procedures so there is full ownership and understanding of the procedures.

3. Establish more focal points, perhaps task forces with designated responsibilities. (Siefert was the focal point for the entire organization.)

4. Establish more upfront communication and training of personnel on the uses, goals, and benefits of registration.

5. Take a little longer. Three plants were initially certified under a fast-track schedule. (Siefert would have pushed out the schedule and dedicated more resources to the project.)

FIRST STEP IN A LONG JOURNEY

The secret of business is constancy of purpose.
—BENJAMIN DISRAELI

A number of W-R employees said that if the rush to become ISO 9000 registered is the first and only consideration of a company then it has the wrong priorities. A company has to think about quality first and then think about ISO 9000 as an important subset of the quality package. The goal may be Malcolm Baldrige–level quality. However, to paraphrase a Confucian pundit, "A long journey starts with the first step." ISO is a giant step in the Total Quality Management journey.

ISO 9000 is not an end unto itself. Siefert says: "You get what you put into it. If you approach ISO 9000 as one of the tools or vehicles for Total Quality Management, a company will get a lot out of it. If it is used as a checklist to satisfy a market need, and if the management effort is not there, then it won't accomplish much for a company."

CHAPTER 10

ISO 9000—Decision Point

Anybody who can look at the business world today and give me a logical explanation for what's going on out there clearly isn't informed.
—CHARLES GARFIELD, Author

The basic question facing your company is: Should you become ISO 9000 registered? A secondary question is: Should you use ISO 9000 criteria as the foundation for a quality system, independent of registration.

The answer is not a simple "yes" or "no." Many factors play into the decision. ISO registration forces a company to focus and to understand its operations and quality systems. You may discover the path—the process of examining the competitiveness issues—surrounding registration will also lead you to examine the basic questions of any business:

- Where am I going?

- Which path will take me there?

- How am I going to get there?

- Who is going to lead or help me?

- How much will it cost?

- Will I get what I want?

197

WHAT CAN ISO REGISTRATION DO FOR YOU?

What can ISO registration or implementation do for you? The following are the reasons offered by most ISO supporters:

- Improves overall competitiveness

- Recognized worldwide

- Provides access to markets

- Enhances marketing credibility

- Establishes production credibility

- Serves as a global TQM model

- Improves supplier base quality

- Creates uniform quality systems

- Improves internal operations

- Avoids duplicative quality audits

- Controls risks and exposures

- Neutralizes competition

- Living documents

- Develops self-discipline

IMPROVES OVERALL COMPETITIVENESS

> *All strategy depends on competition.*
> —BRUCE HENDERSON, CEO,
> Boston Consulting Group

Manufacturing and service businesses have become more complex and competitive. *Quality is globally recognized as an essential ingredient of competitiveness.* It's important that companies have reliable and improving quality management, assurance, and control systems.

The inevitable goal is to enhance an organization's competitiveness through customer satisfaction, continuous improvement, and product innovation. ISO 9000 implementation is often recognized as a first step in the journey. What about further steps in the journey? Higher levels of quality benchmarks or certifications may well be imposed on suppliers as proof of continuous improvement and quality commitment.

RECOGNIZED WORLDWIDE

ISO 9000 registration, CE mark, and other conformity mechanisms can pave the way for selling products across national borders and be used to facilitate global trade. A major reason for EC unification was to provide a harmonized environment where products could move freely and where a governmental entity wouldn't refuse entry if products had been certified by a recognized body.

Safety- and health-related products will carry a CE mark and maybe other certification marks before they have access to the EC market. If the certifying agency is a notified body—accredited by a national authority—audit results sometime in the 1990s should be transparent and comparable throughout the world.

As a market decision, some form of conformity assessment may also become a condition of business for nonregulated products, especially as the marketplace becomes more transparent and customers want higher levels of product or process assurance.

Globalization of ISO 9000

Until recently, products from Hong Kong would be held up by U.S. customs officials because of this absence of proper certifications or approved test data. Improper certifications or lack of test data became barriers to the free movement of products.

Hong Kong is developing the Hong Kong Quality Assurance Agency to carry out ISO 9000 registration. Accepted certifications and/or stamps on products should allow products free movement throughout the world. Already, the U.S., the UK, and Australia are accepting Hong Kong's test data from its accredited laboratories. The inevitable result will be global acceptance of ISO 9000 registration sometime in the 1990s.

Source: M. Slovick, "Hong Kong's Push into High Tech," *Dealership Merchandising*, February 1991, p. 43.

PROVIDES ACCESS TO MARKETS

Becoming ISO 9000 registered can also be a marketing decision. In most cases, registration is voluntary. It can become an important element of a company's marketing effort. As in the decision to pursue the Deming Prize, the European Quality Award, or the Malcolm Baldrige National Quality Award, companies are pursuing registration as a means to position themselves in a crowded marketplace.

Conformance registrations or labels can be used in marketing and promotions. ISO registration or the affixing of the CE mark can promote a company's quality initiative, which should result in increased business for the registered company.

The critical question however is: Why is a company pursuing registration? If it is solely a market-driven need, then it begs the question whether the company has the devotion, stamina, and culture to improve, innovate, and compete continuously.

ENHANCES MARKETING CREDIBILITY

Advertising is a critical mechanism for establishing credibility. This is especially evident with ISO 9000. To position and differentiate themselves, companies are making full-page announcements in trade magazines and newspapers heralding their registration.

Many companies are taking their cue from Ford Motor Company, which advertises in prestigious newspapers the suppliers that have been awarded its highest certification. This is also occurring with the MBNQA winners. Cynics contend that this is a public relations gimmick. The ads don't affect the company's real product or process quality. *However, they inform and obtain the support of key opinion leaders such as the customer's company officers who read the announcements.* ISO 9000 is similarly being elevated as a global seal of quality approval. It demonstrates the company's commitment to quality.

ESTABLISHES PRODUCTION CREDIBILITY

The North American Free Trade Agreement (NAFTA) is encouraging companies to think of moving plants to Mexico to be closer to growing markets and to access cheap labor. One company had a U.S. ISO 9001 registered plant and was transferring production to Mexico. The company sought to register its Mexican plant to ISO 9001.

It wanted to convey the same trust and assurance to its customers that the Mexican plant's products would be made to the same exacting standards as the U.S. ISO 9001 registered plant. If the U.S. company could convince customers, then they would ship products directly from the Mexican plant to the customer's facility and maintain the same level of assurance that U.S. ISO registration afforded them. *This move would deflect some of the stigma of shipping products "Made in Mexico."*

SERVES AS A GLOBAL TQM MODEL

ISO 9004, which is a set of guidelines for internal use, may become the model for future revisions of the contractual ISO 9001, ISO 9002, and ISO 9003. Companies that have improved their quality by registering to 9001 can use ISO 9004 and derivative guideline documents as their next step in the quality-improvement journey.

IMPROVES SUPPLIER BASE QUALITY

If the supplier base, including first-, second-, and lower-tier suppliers are ISO registered, then the final products, which may consist of thousands of parts and components from registered suppliers, should have superior quality, performance, and reliability.

Industry sector suppliers often have to comply with many similar customer quality qualification standards. This is redundant and costly. If a supplier is registered, then existing or prospective customers will check a register to confirm the supplier has the requisite quality systems.

CREATES UNIFORM QUALITY SYSTEMS

Currently, military and regulated industry quality requirements are similar because they are based on MIL-Q 9858A. Regulated and commercial quality has largely diverged. Commercial quality criteria focused on customer satisfaction, continuous improvement, statistical controls, just-in-time, total cost, and other criteria that would enhance a company's competitiveness. During this time, regulatory or military contractors had static, documentation-intensive quality programs largely because they didn't face external competitive pressures. This has now changed.

In the 1990s, external economic circumstances are forcing U.S. military contractors to think and operate commercially and to wean themselves away from guaranteed military contracts. As well, regulated companies must focus on prevention in order to limit their exposure. This is a major leap for military contractors, and some won't be able to develop the requisite commercial quality systems.

The good news is that more regulated companies and military contractors are adopting ISO 9000. Becoming ISO 9000 certified is the first step in their continuous-improvement journey. In the future, ISO 9001/9002/9003 will incorporate more commercial quality criteria.

Also, we're seeing the global convergence of the military, commercial, and other regulatory customer-supplier ISO 9000 registration initiatives. ISO registration is being imposed on even the smallest suppliers and is being used in places such as schools and city government.

IMPROVES INTERNAL OPERATIONS

ISO 9000 standards document quality systems, processes, and procedures. This forces a company to identify what is critical to the customer in terms of requirements, develop procedures to satisfy these requirements, then develop internal systems to monitor, control, and improve quality systems that directly affect customer satisfaction.

The registration process focuses on quality and processes. Hopefully, it results in higher understanding of how operations are running, how they are controlled, and how they can be improved. *In addition, it is a much more defined and disciplined way of doing business thereby improving operational control and flexibility, which is probably the greatest benefit of registration.* Companies often assume operations are in control, capable, and improving. This assumption may be false unless the quality systems are periodically self-audited.

Finally, ISO 9000 also can be used as a platform or as a unified framework to build an extensive and intensive total quality management system.

What If All the People Were Replaced?

What if all the people in a company were replaced? Would the company still be able to produce quality products and deliver quality service? This is often a benchmark question asked by quality auditors.

Its purpose is straightforward. Hypothetically, if quality systems are in place and working properly, and if anyone, supervisor or worker, were replaced or absent, then the existing quality systems would ensure that products and services met specified requirements. For example, the documentation could inform a new employee how to perform a job satisfactorily.

AVOIDS DUPLICATIVE QUALITY AUDITS

Most large companies monitor, evaluate, and certify suppliers through similar formal industry programs. Problems arise when customers audit the same suppliers to the same criteria. It is not unheard of for multiple customer audit teams to revisit the same supplier.

These audits are redundant, looking at the same quality systems, processes, and products. The customer must send an audit team to the supplier, resulting in transportation, salary, and other costs. The supplier must assign individuals to support the customer's audit team as well as rearrange internal operations so auditors can observe processes, tests, or inspections.

If a supplier is on a general or an industry-specific register, then an existing or prospective customer can check the registry to determine compliance with one of the ISO 9000 quality standards. To compete in certain markets or to supply a well-known organization, suppliers must demonstrate they are "world class." ISO 9000 certification process is a threshold indicator of a company's commitment to pursue world-class standing. Another advantage of ISO 9000 registration is it becomes an opportunity to develop a customer-supplier partnership.

CONTROLS RISKS AND EXPOSURES

> *You may never achieve zero defects. But if you want to avoid lawsuits,*
> *try to reach that goal.*
> —MARISA MANLEY, Attorney

All U.S. manufacturers are aware of the costs and risks associated with litigation. One accident can put a small organization at risk. One of the more powerful drivers for ISO 9000 registration is to ensure a supplier has the minimum requisite quality systems.

If there should be product liability litigation, a product audit trail may not guarantee products are defect free. *However, extensive quality systems, in place and operating properly, should minimize the possibility of future failures and give the customer some assurance that defects won't occur or recur.* It may also avoid or minimize damage claims.

This assurance becomes more important as companies focus on their core strengths and outsource more operations. A large percentage of the manufacturing dollar is invested in procured parts and assemblies. The sources may be domestic or foreign. As well, the sources of some critical parts may be two or more tiers removed from the final manufacturer or assembler. Or the manufacturer may purchase parts from a distributor that obtains offshore components.

In these circumstances, the customer/buyer wants to know and be assured that products comply with requirements. There is a tremendous need for harmonized standards, conformity assessment, and certification assurance.

NEUTRALIZES COMPETITION

Another legitimate purpose of registration is competitive damage control. *Many companies with sophisticated quality programs that surpass ISO 9000 requirements are pursuing registration only to neutralize a competitor's market advantage.* Companies don't want their competition to use it as a means to enhance reputations at their expense or to access markets that are denied to them.

In some cases, there may be little direct value added to registration. A company may already have advanced quality systems, and its only reason to register is to enter markets, seek parity with competition, or appease customers requiring registration. If the competition is using it for credibility or marketability purposes, then a company may be left out of the bidding loop purely for not having a piece of paper.

LIVING DOCUMENTS

ISO 9000 will probably be revised in 1996–97 to include quality planning, continuous improvement, and measurement. Proceduralizing does not necessarily mean the quality system is static. Internal documents will evolve over time

---

Negotiate, Don't Litigate

The Europeans are less litigious than Americans. But this may change. In 1988 an EC directive set strict corporate liability governing when the consumer can sue a supplier if its goods or services are found to be faulty or dangerous. It is going to become much easier to successfully sue a company or supplier under the new regulations.

It's presumed in the EC that adherence to quality systems will protect suppliers and companies. One registrar maintains that "in the event of a prosecution, evidence of compliance with (quality) standards may help a company refute allegations of negligence by demonstrating that all reasonable steps were taken to control the production processes in a proper manner."*

* BVQI (Bureau Veritas Registrar) marketing brochure, 1992.

---

to reflect new and better operational methods as well as the new ISO requirements.

DEVELOPS SELF-DISCIPLINE

Show me a man who cannot be bothered to do little things and I'll show you a man who cannot be trusted to do the big things.
—LAWRENCE BELL,
Helicopter Designer

ISO 9000 implementation is about doing the little things right. If enough little things are accomplished well, the larger goals such as customer satisfaction, product innovation, continuous improvement should be achievable.

ISO 9000 forces self-discipline in terms of identifying customer needs, then taking the information internally to develop recommended or mandatory procedures, standards, and practices. A fundamental element of the commonly accepted quality gospel is the ability to define and follow these practices. This ability results in products that are more consistent and therefore have higher quality.

Against these advantages and benefits you'll have to weigh the challenges to registration. Some of the imposing ones are discussed in the next section.

REGISTRATION AND AUDITING CHALLENGES

*Today, loving change, tumult, even chaos is a prerequisite for survival,
let alone success.*
                                                    —TOM PETERS

ISO registration involves allocating time, personnel, dollars, and other resources.
All of which are scarce in these constrained times. Often, people are not hired to
pursue registration. It is simply placed on top of everything else that workers
need to do. Next, we examine the following constraints and challenges to
registration:

- Increased government involvement

- Political confusion

- Overcertification

- Adding cost, not value

- Credibility loss

- No guarantee of customer satisfaction or product quality

- Hype and hoopla

- Registration dismissal

- Appearance of conflicts of interest

- Variation in auditor quality

- Differences in interpreting ISO 9000 standards

- Documentation does not satisfy customers

- Hindering creativity and innovation

- Lack of understanding of purposes and goals of conformity
  assessment

- No emphasis on continuous improvement

- Overpromise and underdeliver

Increased Government Involvement

The U.S. government will be more involved in standards development and conformity assessment issues in the 1990s. Standards making has become a public-policy issue dealing with foreign trade and competitiveness.

The U.S. government has a legitimate role in standards development and implementation. Domestically, the government can encourage interagency standard development, cooperation, and coordination. Internationally, the U.S. government can represent American industry positions and negotiate with EC-member states' standards and testing organizations for mutual recognition of test results.

Political Confusion

The process of conformity assessment is moving slowly in the EC and U.S. due to political and economic pressures, which specifically are:

- EC political and economic integration has been stymied through EC-member votes.

- Reciprocal testing and certification recognition is limited outside the EC.

- EC standards development is proceeding slowly.

- National protectionist pressures may delay the process.

- Trade flow may become disrupted and result in further trade disputes.

- U.S. conformity assessment is following an industry consensual process.

Overcertification

The Europeans are regulating many elements of their citizens' life, from environment, safety, consumer products, waste, quality-of-work life, and the list goes on. With a Democratic House and Administration, the U.S. government will probably become more actively involved in quality and the pursuit and maintenance of the quality of work, family, and environmental life. And there is a possibility that commerce may become overly regimented through multiple regulations and certifications. *A product may conceivably carry environmental, customer, regulatory, and other certification labels.* Overcertification, at that point, does not add value but is simply a reaction to the laissez-faire conditions of previous administrations.

ADDING COST, NOT VALUE

The refrain "ISO 9000 registration is just so much paperwork, and it does not add value to my operations" is often heard! And sometimes it is true. ISO 9000 registration is costly and paperwork intensive. Many resources are expended. However, if a company wants to do business overseas or with large companies in either the regulated or nonregulated sectors, registration may well become a cost of doing business.

Is this process based on reason or value? No. Often it is a herd mentality where the perception is that registration is mandatory. And as with any self-fulfilling prophecy, it becomes so.

CREDIBILITY LOSS

What happens when a customer shops registrars and goes to the easiest or cheapest? Registration does follow the market and as such it is acceptable. What is unacceptable is the implicit promise "If you use my company, you'll become registered." *The self-regulated registration process can conceivably break down and self-destruct.* Due diligence and proper safeguards may not be followed. Auditors cut corners. Trust is broken. The entire registration process becomes meaningless.

According to some sources, this has already occurred in the EC where some accreditors and laboratories are more credible and therefore better than those of other EC-member nations. What occurs is that a hierarchy of quality certification and testing agencies evolves that can destroy the premise of transparency and mutual recognition of certification and test results.

NO GUARANTEE OF CUSTOMER SATISFACTION OR PRODUCT QUALITY

> *Read through the course catalog of an average business school. Sit through the local success seminar. You hear a whole lot more about process than about product.*
> —ELLEN GOODMAN, Writer

Quality systems, not products, are registered. This is an important distinction. The assumption is if quality systems exist, internal processes are controlled. A further assumption is if they are controlled, they are capable and are improving. Finally, the products from these processes conform to customer requirements.

This may well be a stretch. *Having registered quality systems can be far removed from guaranteeing product quality or satisfying customers.*

Hype and Hoopla

> *There's no such thing as a free lunch.*
> —Milton Friedman, Economist

The biggest external problem with ISO 9000 registration is that it is perceived as a panacea for quality or competitiveness. There is a tremendous worldwide demand for becoming competitive; however, of the millions of companies worldwide, only thousands have become registered and only tens of thousands are even aware of its existence. And, as more companies believe the road to competitiveness starts with registration, more will pursue it.

The hoopla surrounding ISO 9000 is stunning. ISO 9001 is a seven-page threshold quality document. Is interest in the standard the result of the growth in the quality-management movement, or is it the perception that ISO registration is the silver bullet that will make companies instantly competitive? Registration with commitment and effort is doable. However, the decisions required for securing competitiveness are often painful.

Jim Highlands, president of Management Systems Analysis and a U.S. TAG member to TC 176, explains an interesting phenomenon surrounding registration:

> The current conformity assessment scheme is analogous to paying the IRS $30,000 for a continuous three-year audit of your tax returns. Where there is little question of its need for high-risk products, such as medical devices, it is currently being foisted onto much of U.S. industry as *real quality*. The problem with U.S. industry is that we believe that all problems can be solved if we just attend one more seminar. Relief is just a swallow away, or perhaps an assessment away. MBO, quality circles, SPC, CIP, TQM, and conformity assessment will solve all our problems. It's like watching a juicer demonstration and thinking instant health is just a carrot away.

Registration Dismissal

Some totally dismiss ISO 9000. They say: "I have seen this before and this too shall pass." The number of programs and alphabet soup are long.

ISO 9000 ignorance is dangerous and may be disastrous. If a company wants to do business in Europe, a company may find it has to become part of the contract or purchase order boilerplate. While ISO registration or a similar conformity assessment was intended to address safety requirements in regulated industries, its use is increasingly expanding to cover unregulated industries, military contractors, and other industry sectors, so conceivably it becomes a condition to business.

There is a very real urgency with ISO 9000 registration. Some companies whose products were targeted by a specific directive didn't pursue registration in the U.S. or overseas, and if it was, it was pursued grudgingly. One small instrumentation manufacturer is now desperately registering all its plants. It did not understand the implications of the particular directive that required products connecting with the European Telecommunications Network to be purchased from manufacturers that have been ISO 9000 registered.

APPEARANCE OF CONFLICTS OF INTEREST

The appearance of conflict of interest is a problem with some registrars. Registration audits are supposed to be conducted by independent third parties. However, the third parties are in the business to generate revenue, and most registrars compete and advertise heavily for auditing and consulting services. These registrars will conduct the audit and also provide consulting services during the preassessment and the audit. They say they maintain independence and impartiality by separating the auditing and consulting functions within the organization. Yes, but both functions in small registrar companies still report to the same person who may conduct audits and consult with a company simultaneously.

VARIATION IN AUDITOR QUALITY

Gresham's Law says: "Bad money drives out good money." Well, *Hutchins's Law of Quality Auditing says: "Bad quality auditors drive out good auditors."* And, the corollary: "Bad audits result in litigation and conformity assessment diminution."

A major problem in the quality-auditing community is the high variation in auditor quality. Again, consistency and uniformity in training, education, and implementation are hallmarks of quality. This sometimes seems to be lacking in the quality-auditing community. There is tremendous demand for quality auditors. Their supply is relatively small, and there are few barriers to entry. Quality auditors sometimes don't have sufficiently extensive and intensive quality backgrounds. They don't have specific process or product backgrounds, which may result in an auditor focusing on the trivial and missing the critical factors during an audit. Inexperienced auditors are answering yes/no questions from a checklist, seeing but not understanding what is occurring in front of them. This rote method of simply checking responses is a major problem with compliance type of audits such as ISO 9000.

The Registrar Accreditation Board has developed training and education requirements for becoming a lead auditor. These requirements are generic, so many quality auditors still won't have the requisite background to conduct an industry-, process-, or product-specific audit. To address this problem, one auditor on a team should have an industry-specific background while other team members have generic auditing backgrounds. Unfortunately, the issue of inadequately trained auditors won't be resolved until auditors and registrars are legally accountable for the consequential results of their decisions.

DIFFERENCES IN INTERPRETING ISO 9000 STANDARDS

Auditors interpret the ISO standards differently. For example, ISO 9001 requires an auditor to verify a manufacturer's systems for evaluating purchased materials. However, the manufacturer's compliance may be through statistical process control charts or through inspection.

DOCUMENTATION DOES NOT SATISFY CUSTOMERS

Quality systems thinking, to some, implies documentation and paperwork thinking. Documentation is an outgrowth of quality systems control, but is not an end to itself. The quality manual should not be developed to only appease the customer that the requisite quality systems are in place and working.

HINDERING CREATIVITY AND INNOVATION

A downside to defining and proceduralizing operations may be to deny a person's initiative and creativity. Some say the amount of paperwork forces repetition and uniformity at a high organizational cost. Designers and research/development scientists may view standards as an unnecessary imposition and a hindrance to their creativity.

There is a fine line in developing procedures that describe required or acceptable actions that won't limit initiative and innovation. In terms of complying with ISO 9000, one tack sometimes followed by organizations with a culture of freedom and creativity is to develop procedures to comply with the intent of ISO 9000 language. In many cases, the particular ISO 9000 section leaves some latitude with respect to compliance. As long as the company complies with the intent of the language and the customer and auditor share a common understanding of the language, the auditor should indicate conformance.

Another problem is that ISO procedures may be imposed on workers as the "approved" operating method. This can occur when outsiders, consultants, or corporate staff develop procedures in a vacuum and do not discuss them with the workers. The best solution is to have workers write their own ISO procedures. This makes sense because they are best acquainted with how the work is actually done. Staff may serve as consultant and aid the effort. Another obstacle to be overcome is the natural suspicion of "they want to find out what I do so they (management) can find someone cheaper." Another challenge is that many people don't know how to write procedures. And, finally, building consensus for a team or work area to write procedures takes time.

LACK OF UNDERSTANDING OF PURPOSES AND GOALS OF CONFORMITY ASSESSMENT

The decision to seek registration is not easy and can be costly. To decide whether to seek registration, it is important to understand how EC directives will affect a company. These directives address specific industry sectors and require specific actions to demonstrate conformance. It's important to track EC directives and the latest conformity assessment initiatives.

How do you know if a product is targeted for conformity assessment? There are several ways. One is to identify the directives that apply to your industry. Second, talk to customers and competitors and ask if they anticipate ISO registration in the near future. Finally, talk with people who operate overseas and identify which industry sectors are targeted for registration or are shielded from foreign competition.[1]

[1] R. Williams, M. Teagan, and J. Beneyton, *The World's Largest Market*, New York, NY: Amacom, 1990, pp. 24–25.

No Emphasis on Continuous Improvement

ISO 9000 auditing does not emphasize continuous improvement. The auditor may issue a Corrective Action Request. However, the corrective action does not address how the problem will be corrected. In the follow-up surveillance audit, the auditor may reaudit the corrective action or investigate if the problem recurred. However, the ISO audit is not an audit of customer satisfaction or continuous improvement.

The best the ISO quality auditor can do is to assess the auditee's internal quality auditing systems. In this way, the ISO auditor can determine if problems have recurred or if there are unusual deficiency patterns.

Overpromise and Underdeliver

Quality auditing is perceived by some as the "full employment act of the quality professional." As one auditor aspirant said: "This is the hottest thing since the Malcolm Baldrige." This attitude can create major problems for the credibility of ISO registration in terms of people in the field overpromising or overestimating the value of registration.

"LEAD, FOLLOW, OR GET OUT OF THE WAY"

Concentrate your strength against your competitor's relative weakness.
—Bruce Henderson, CEO,
Boston Consulting Group

One of the toughest things in writing a book is to distill everything that has been written in one pithy paragraph or section. The decision to seek registration can be summed up as a matter of "lead, follow, or get out of the way."

Bill Cromer, quality director of White-Rodgers, singled out the following as the biggest benefit to ISO 9000 registration:

You basically sign up to hold your feet to the fire to establish and maintain your quality systems. A company-wide quality improvement process is something that everyone is going to do eventually. The only question you're going to ask is: "Are you going to lead, follow, or get out of the way." In other words, are you going to jump on this when it's early and make your competitors run to catch up, or are you going to sit around and wait until you have to run to catch up. To some extent, it's the same with ISO 9000. In our case, we got on it first and now our competitors are running to catch up, and it isn't so easy. All the time you're working on it, they don't even know you're working on it. And when you hit the news with it, now you're two years ahead of them and they've got to scramble. And, they know you're out there using it to your advantage.[2]

FINAL THOUGHTS

The competitive urge is a fine, wholesome direction of energy. But . . .
the desire to win must be wedded to an ideal, an ethical way of life. It
must never become so strong that it dwarfs every other aspect of the
game of life.

—EDWARD R. MURROW

Regardless of what the quality prophets say, the future of conformity assessment and ISO 9000 is still uncertain because these assurance mechanisms are, in the end, political and economic instruments.

We've speculated how the world will look in the post–Cold War. Will it consist of trading blocs or tribal nations? Will it consist of managed, free, or protected trade? I don't know the answer. However, ISO 9000 and other international standards can serve multiple economic and political purposes. On one hand, they can be used to open up trade and make product standards transparent. Or they can be used as punitive instruments or as hurdles to restrict trade. If the world becomes clusters of trading blocs, then standards may become mechanisms to free intrabloc trade and to manage interbloc trade. The issue again is still cloudy, and ISO 9000's future is not totally clear and depends on the nature of future trade.

John Culbertson, the economist, sums it up well: "What is reasonably sought is not a system of foreign trade that would work in a visionary world of homogeneous nations acting out a script from laissez-faire economics, but a system of foreign trade that will work constructively and bring mutually beneficial trade between nations when these nations continue to differ from one another in innumerable ways, including their industrial policies and their trade policies."[3]

---

[2] Personal communication

[3] J. Culbertson, *The Trade Threat* (Madison, WI: 21st Century Press, 1989), p. 9.

Value and Trust

At a national level, the future of ISO 9000 and in a larger context, conformity assessment, can be summed up by three key words: credibility, value, and trust. National conformity assessment structures are still at the infant stage. They have not yet earned their credibility.

National conformity assessment structures are rising throughout the world as well as in the U.S. In the U.S., the government is proposing active involvement in the regulated industry sectors, and the Registration Accreditation Board is actively pursuing similar activities in regulated and nonregulated sectors. As well, each ISO signatory is developing its own national laboratory and test accreditation and certification schemes. As long as there are slight variations among these, then the long-term prospects for establishing a net of Mutual Recognition Agreements ensuring global product transparency are very good. However, if each nation establishes distinctly different conformity structures, then there may well be increased variation among national test and certification results, thus ensuring loss of trust.

European Experience

The European experience offers glimpses of what other nations, trading blocs, and the world may expect in terms of conformity assessment. The EC has been attempting to harmonize its diverse national conformity structures for some time. The pace has been unexpectedly slow as each conformity assessment stakeholder attempts to protect its position.

B. Sjoberg, managing director of SEMKO, one of Europe's major electrotechnical testing and certification bodies, recently said: "When the markets do not trust [the conformity assessment process], there is no point in trying to tell them that you should trust the process because trust is something that you have to earn. It cannot be imposed."[4]

How will U.S. conformity assessment mechanisms work? Again, it comes back to the three key words: *value, credibility*, and *trust*. What will determine its utility in the U.S.? The marketplace. Who will determine its usability in the world? The politicians and economists.

[4] B. Sjoberg, "Testing and Certification in Europe: The Role for EOTC," workshop proceeding, Brussels, Belgium: EOTC, 1992.

APPENDIX

Sample Quality Manual

The following is Quality Manufacturing's (a fictitious company) quality manual that is based on ISO 9001—1987's twenty quality elements. There is a one-to-one correspondence between the ISO 9001 quality systems and the policies in this sample quality manual.

The quality manual is often the core document needed for registration. The registrar's auditors review it to ensure that all the quality system elements of the standard are addressed. By reviewing the following material, you can obtain an understanding of the critical points of the standards.

Several points should first be reviewed. ISO 9001, which is only seven pages, is the most comprehensive contractual quality ISO 9000 standard. This quality manual is longer than the standard because it specifically details actions by which the standard can be complied. In some of the quality systems, the detailed manual describes actions that are consistent with but go beyond the requirements of ISO 9001.

If you are starting the ISO registration process, you can use it as the core outline for your manual. For your specific process and product needs, the manual will probably have to be tailored.

QUALITY MANUFACTURING'S CORPORATE MISSION STATEMENT

Quality Manufacturing (QM) believes and follows the precepts of Total Quality Management as detailed in ISO 9001. Prevention and continuous improvement are the fundamental elements to securing and maintaining total customer satisfaction. Each employee of Quality Manufacturing is accountable for ensuring that external and internal customers are satisfied and will follow the quality systems and procedures detailed in this quality manual.

The quality assurance organization is responsible for maintaining and updating this manual. Each organizational head is accountable for ensuring that all quality systems and procedures are followed.

JOHN BROWN
Chief Executive Officer

ISO 9001: 4.1
MANAGEMENT RESPONSIBILITY

1.0 **Quality Policy.** QM anticipates and exceeds customer's requirements and expectations through cost-competitive quality products and services that are delivered on time, every time.

1.1 QM's executive management is totally committed to total customer satisfaction through cost-competitive quality products and services.

2.0 **Organization.** QM's personnel have the authority and responsibility to maintain, implement, and update QM's quality system. This includes:
- initiating corrective action to prevent nonconformances
- identifying and recording nonconformances
- initiating changes to eliminate symptoms and root causes
- verifying effectiveness of corrective action

2.1 All QM personnel are responsible for verifying system and product compliance to QM policies and procedures. Quality systems auditing is conducted of all company operations by independent and objective individuals.

2.2 QM has a management representative responsible for maintaining and ensuring ISO 9001 quality system registration. The corporate representative is Jane Smith. The business unit person is the quality vice president. The plant person is the quality assurance manager.

3.0 **Management Review of Quality Systems.** QM's quality policies, procedures, and overall quality system are periodically reviewed by management and audited by business-unit and plant-designated personnel.

3.1 The overall Total Quality Management system is audited and reviewed at the corporate, business unit, and plant levels at least once a year. The head of quality at each organizational level is responsible for the audit.

The review covers:
- complete, current, and accurate specifications
- application of procedures
- quality manual completeness
- corrective action effectiveness

Management reviews quality strategic plans, tactical plans, accountabilities, policies, procedures, and benchmarks to improve operational effectiveness, efficiency, and economy.

ISO 9001: 4.2
QUALITY SYSTEM

1.0 **Quality System.** QM maintains an organization, personnel, and quality systems to ensure external and internal customer satisfaction through cost-competitive quality products and services.

1.1 QM maintains Total Quality Management systems to ensure internal and external customer satisfaction in its products and services.

Quality accountabilities and authorities have been assigned for developing, maintaining, monitoring, measuring, and improving quality activities.

1.2 ISO 9001 forms the foundation and structure of all QM's quality systems.

1.3 QM's quality systems are certified and registered by Quality Science Registrars. QM notifies the registrar of significant quality system changes. The quality officer of the appropriate organizational level is responsible for notifying the registrar.

2.0 **System Documentation.** Quality systems documentation includes quality policies, procedures, work instructions, and other documentation. ISO 9001 quality policies and procedures are incorporated into the quality manual.

2.1 Quality manual numbering corresponds to ISO 9001.

3.0 **Quality Plan.** QM has plans to ensure operational consistency and prevent nonconformances. Quality analysis planning involves all operations personnel, including professional, administrative, service, and production. The goal of quality planning is to ensure customer satisfaction through the delivery of quality products and services.

4.0 **Quality Records.** Quality documentation is maintained according to quality procedures.

5.0 **Responsibility.** The chief quality officer of the operational unit is responsible for ensuring that quality procedures are monitored and improved. All employees are responsible for following quality procedures and for continuous, measurable improvement.

5.1 QM quality management reviews quality policies, systems, procedures, and documentation. Quality audits and reviews focus on efficiency, effectiveness, and economy.

ISO 9001: 4.3
CONTRACT REVIEW

1.0 **Contract Requirements.** Customer documents and contracts are reviewed prior to acceptance to ensure that customer requirements are defined and understood.

The following contractual quality documentation are periodically reviewed:
- purchase orders
- product and process specifications
- quality plans
- control and capability requirements

2.0 **Customer Contract Review.** New or modified products are reviewed to ensure:
- requirements are defined and understood
- new requirements can be complied

3.0 **New Product Development.** Customer satisfaction, defect prevention, and continuous improvement are key elements of new product development.

4.0 **Capabilities.** Existing and new product contracts are evaluated in terms of QM's ability to satisfy customer requirements. Equipment, environment, personnel, engineering, manufacturing, methods, tooling, and other systems are evaluated.

5.0 **Records.** Contract review records are maintained and accessible by all parties.

ISO 9001: 4.4
DESIGN CONTROL

1.0 **Design Development and Planning.** Designs are controlled and planned throughout product development to ensure that specified requirements are satisfied. Design output and input variables are identified, controlled, monitored, measured, and documented throughout product development.

1.1 Product design and verification activities are planned by and assigned to quality representatives for review.

1.2 Design control information is documented, communicated, and reviewed throughout product development.

2.0 **Design Input.** Product requirements are identified and documented. Groups with specific expertise who can contribute are identified.

3.0 **Design Output.** Design output is documented in terms of satisfying customer requirements by:
- defining process and product requirements
- containing acceptance criteria
- conforming to industry requirements or government regulations
- classifying and prioritizing product attributes that deal with safety, health, consumer protection, or environmental conditions

4.0 **Design Verification.** Designs are planned, documented, and verified throughout the product-development process. Design verification involves the following:
- holding design reviews
- conducting reliability testing
- analyzing design calculations
- comparing designs against competitor's products
- conducting independent analysis
- reviewing safety and health issues

5.0 **Design Changes.** Design modifications, changes, or revisions are monitored, controlled, verified, and documented through the Engineering Change Order (ECO) system. The ECO system is close-looped so that it identifies changes, permits reviews of the changes, and secures approvals.

ISO 9001: 4.5
DOCUMENT CONTROL

1.0 **Approval and Issue.** Quality systems are documented and controlled. Control involves the issue, approval, review, distribution, and modification of documents.

1.1 Documents are available at appropriate operational locations involving quality systems.

2.0 **Changes and Modifications.** Documentation changes and modifications are recorded to ensure prompt action.

ISO 9001: 4.6
PURCHASING

1.0 **Selection of Suppliers.** Suppliers of products and services are selected, monitored, and improved through specified requirements involving quality, delivery, service, and cost.

1.1 Suppliers are selected based on the following criteria:
- past history
- process control
- site audit
- self-assessment
- product inspection and testing
- performance history
- reliability, maintainability, and other testing

1.2 Each business unit maintains and evaluates records of supplier performance.

2.0 **Purchased Data and Documentation.** Purchasing information is documented and current, complete, and accurate.

2.1 All purchasing and customer documentation is retained, including:
- purchase order
- engineering prints
- supplier evaluation forms
- product test data.

2.2 QM quality representatives review and approve all customer and supplier documentation throughout product development and product life cycles.

2.3 Customer requirements and expectations are fully described in documentation, including:
- type, number, level, and other data of required materials

- type of services
- acceptance levels
- delivery requirements
- costs
- performance requirements
- engineering and manufacturing process
- corrective actions.

ISO 9001: 4.7
PURCHASER SUPPLIED PRODUCTS

1.0 **Procedures.** Procedures are established for specifying, identifying, transporting, and storing purchased materials.

1.1 Qualified stores' personnel identify, count, and verify that supplied materials conform to contract and quality requirements. Conforming and nonconforming materials are segregated, stored, handled, and tagged according to procedures.

1.2 Purchased materials are stored, handled, and transported according to approved procedures and industry standards.

2.0 **Lost, Damaged, or Unsuitable Materials.** Lost, damaged, or unsuitable materials are documented and reported to the customer.

ISO 9001: 4.8
PRODUCT IDENTIFICATION AND TRACEABILITY

1.0 **Material and Product Identification.** Procedures are established and maintained to identify and document materials and products throughout product development and the product life cycle.

2.0 **Traceability.** In-house and purchased materials are traced through product development and the product life cycles. Traceability also extends to delivery and installation.

ISO 9001: 4.9
PROCESS CONTROL

1.0 **General Processes.** All major organizational processes are controlled. If applicable, processes are in control and capable.

1.1 Process control includes documented procedures, trained employees, statistically controlled machinery, monitored environments, and calibrated equipment. Procedures and work instructions are developed for each job, and employees understand responsibilities. Quality systems are evaluated periodically to ensure that they are current, accurate, and complete. Internal customer satisfaction is also monitored.

2.0 **Special Processes.** Special processes are those that are operator dependent.

2.1 Special processes are monitored and controlled.

2.2 Process control requirements are defined for all process variables.

2.3 Outputs from special processes are monitored to ensure that they comply with specifications, procedures, and instructions.

2.4 Records are maintained and available for special processes, equipment, and personnel.

ISO 9001: 4.10
INSPECTION AND TESTING

1.0 **Receiving Inspection and Testing.** Materials and products are inspected according to documented procedures that ensure conformance to specifications.

1.1 Receiving inspection ensures that incoming materials conform to quality specifications. If materials cannot or are not inspected, then certifications of compliance may be required from the supplier. Materials from certified suppliers are not inspected.

1.2 The quality organization is responsible for generating and controlling inspection reports and other supplier quality documentation.

1.3 First-item sample products from suppliers are evaluated by the quality and engineering organizations. Results are communicated to Purchasing for supplier approval.

First-item samples must be received and evaluated prior to production. First-item samples are required for new products, modifications of existing products, new suppliers, or new processes.

Engineering, Quality, Manufacturing, and Purchasing must sign off on the first-item samples. Upon acceptance, an approval document is generated with test results. Purchasing is responsible for communicating approval to the supplier.

If the sample is rejected, all documentation is sent to Purchasing, who communicates the reasons and alternatives to the supplier.

1.4 If material is urgently required, Engineering, Quality, Manufacturing, and Purchasing jointly approve the waiver.

2.0 **In-process Inspection and Testing.** In-process testing and inspection stations are identified on a flow chart or similar document. Supplementary documentation identifies type of inspection, product characteristics, inspection methods, inspection levels, AQLs, and inspection equipment.

3.0 **Final Inspection and Testing.** Final testing and inspection stations are identified on a flow chart or similar document. Supplementary documentation identifies type of inspection, product characteristics, inspection methods, inspection levels, AQLs, and inspection equipment.

4.0 **Inspection and Test Records.** Inspection and test records are maintained and indicate conformance.

ISO 9001: 4.11
INSPECTION, MEASURING, AND TEST EQUIPMENT

1.0 **General Requirements.** During product development, key product characteristics are identified on engineering prints or similar documents. Inspection, measuring, and test equipment are identified to measure the previously indicated product characteristics accurately and precisely.

 Inspection, measurement, and test equipment are calibrated for precision and accuracy. Calibration status is recorded on the gauge and on quality documentation.

 In-house reference calibration is conducted in controlled conditions.

 Inspection, measurement, and tests are all proceduralized.

 Internal reference gauges and external calibration services are transferable to NIST.

2.0 **Responsibilities.** Responsibilities for inspection, measurement, and testing are detailed.

 Organizational personnel are responsible for checking and ensuring accurate and precise measurement equipment. Measurement equipment is stored, handled, and secured according to procedures.

3.0 **Specific Requirements.** The following are specific requirements for measurement equipment:
- equipment is properly identified
- location, calibration date, calibration frequency, authority, and other criteria are documented

- damaged or uncalibrated equipment is segregated
- calibration processes are evaluated

ISO 9001: 4.12
INSPECTION AND TEST STATUS

1.0 **Identification.** Inspection and test status of products is identified throughout production. Nonconforming products are properly tagged and segregated. Conforming products are only released to the next production step if identification indicates proper release status. Identification must follow procedures and may include tags, labels, or marks.

2.0 **Authority.** Release authority for conforming products are identified on products, lots, or shipments.

ISO 9001: 4.13
CONTROL OF NONCONFORMING PRODUCT

1.0 **Control of Nonconforming Material and Products.** Nonconforming products are identified, evaluated, segregated, and disposed of according to procedures.

2.0 **Review and Inspection.** Nonconforming materials are reviewed according to procedures. They may be:
- scrapped
- reworked
- used as is
- returned to supplier
- regraded.

3.0 **Records.** Nonconforming products are retained or disposed of according to procedures. Records are maintained of any actions dealing with materials.

ISO 9001: 4.14
CORRECTIVE ACTION

1.0 **Purpose.** Corrective action is planned and documented. Corrective action focuses on eliminating the symptom and the root cause.

2.0 **Investigation and Analysis.** Nonconformances, flaws, or deficiencies are prioritized, and the most significant are analyzed and eliminated first. Some of the analysis tools used are cost of quality, SPC, customer complaints, and inspection results.

3.0 **Prevention and Control Actions.** The goal of corrective action is to prevent recurrences. The results of corrective action are investigated to ensure that problems do not recur.

4.0 **Documentation and Records.** Corrective action from initiation to result is documented properly.

ISO 9001: 4.15
HANDLING, STORAGE, PACKAGING, AND DELIVERY

1.0 **General Procedures.** Production materials are identified so there is an audit trail from incoming material to customer delivery or to final disposition. Procedures are developed for handling, storing, packaging, and delivering materials.

2.0 **Handling.** Handling procedures ensure that materials are not damaged through the production cycle. Procedures and drawings prescribe proper containers. Procedures also detail special handling requirements.

3.0 **Storage.** Storage procedures ensure that materials are not damaged through the production cycle. Storage procedures specially instruct personnel on maintaining proper environmental conditions.

4.0 **Packaging.** Packaging procedures ensure that materials are not damaged throughout the production cycle. Packaging is designed to meet customer requirements, type of transportation, product, cost, and other factors.

5.0 **Delivery.** Delivery procedures ensure that materials are not damaged during internal or external transit. Packaging accounts for misuse or abuse so materials still conform to requirements.

ISO 9001: 4.16
QUALITY RECORDS

1.0 **General Requirements.** Quality records are generated and maintained throughout the organization for all critical activities and functions. Quality records can be retrieved easily and are available to all personnel.

Quality records are identifiable, accurate, complete, and current. Quality records are traceable and auditable to processes, products, results.

2.0 **Records Types.** Many types of quality records are retained, including:

- specifications
- quality costs
- supplier quality
- inspection and measurement
- internal audits
- design review
- customer complaints
- process quality
- product performance
- corrective actions
- audit results.

3.0 **Retention.** Quality records are retained according to specific requirements in procedures and policies.

ISO 9001: 4.17
INTERNAL QUALITY AUDITS

1.0 **Audit Schedule.** Quality audits are prioritized based on importance, cost, and internal requirements.

2.0 **Audit Specific Requirements.** The quality organization is responsible for planning, conducting, and reporting audit results. Quality audits are conducted by independent, trained, and qualified personnel. Audits follow procedures. The organization, processes, systems, or products are audited.

3.0 **Results.** Audit reports are distributed to the specified people defined in procedures. Audited areas may be reaudited to evaluate efficiency, effectiveness, and economy of corrective action.

3.1 The entire organization, business units, and plants are audited yearly to determine compliance with policies and procedures.

ISO 9001: 4.18
TRAINING

1.0 **General Requirements.** All employees are trained to do jobs properly so the internal and ultimately the external customer are satisfied. Job requirements are spelled out to perform the required work.

2.0 **Quality Training.** Quality is an essential element of the training and development of new and existing employees. Training efforts are periodically evaluated and updated. Critical elements of quality training are:

- external and internal customer satisfaction is critical

- customers are satisfied through Total Quality Management
- prevention and continuous improvement are required to keep up with changing customer expectations
- benchmarks are established, and progress is measured
- suppliers are important partners in the process

3.0 **Responsibilities.** Operational and functional area heads are responsible for ensuring that training and development objectives are attained.

4.0 **Records.** Training records are maintained for all employees.

5.0 **Training Programs.** Quality training is industry, company, process, and product specific.

ISO 9001: 4.19
SERVICING

1.0 **General Requirements.** Service processes, systems, and documentation properly address service requirements. After-sales service is documented so the customer requirements are satisfied. Internal and external customers are surveyed to determine customer satisfaction.

2.0 **Responsibilities.** Customer service accountabilities are defined for all appropriate personnel.

3.0 **Records.** Service records, including survey results, failure modes, costs, and studies, are maintained and periodically assessed.

ISO 9001: 4.20
STATISTICAL TECHNIQUES

1.0 **General Requirements.** Statistical techniques are established for appropriate business processes. Personnel are trained in statistical prevention. Records are maintained to record the results of statistical analysis and to pursue continuous improvement.

2.0 **Sampling Plans.** Sampling and inspection plans reflect supplier's process capabilities, type of products, product characteristics, costs, and risks.

3.0 **Techniques.** The list of statistical techniques includes but is not limited to the following:
- Statistical Process Control (SPC)
- Taguchi methods
- histograms
- reliability calculations

- engineering calculations
- sampling

4.0 **Applications.** Statistical analysis is used in the following:
- reliability testing
- production processes
- engineering product development
- market analysis
- continuous improvement
- customer satisfaction

GLOSSARY

Accreditation. Procedure by which an authoritative body recognizes the competence of a group to conduct registration activities, tests, or other conformity assessment activities.

ANSI. Acronym for American National Standards Institute; nonprofit standards-development organization; ISO member.

ASQC. Acronym for American Society for Quality Control (USA); consists of more than 100,000 quality management, assurance, and control professionals.

Audit preassessment. Evaluation prior to quality systems audit to determine the auditee's readiness; usually involves analysis of auditee's quality documentation.

Auditee. Organization or area being audited.

Auditor. Also called quality auditor or quality assessor; person qualified to conduct quality systems audits.

Bilateral recognition. Agreement between two parties to accept each others' conformity assessment results; also called bilateral arrangement; *see* mutual recognition.

BSi. Acronym for British Standards Institute; quasi-government and private British standards-making organization.

CAR. Acronym for Corrective Action Request; conclusion by quality systems auditor to have auditee correct deficiency in an ISO requirement.

CE mark. Protected mark indicating conformance to all EC directive requirements.

CEN/CENELEC. CEN is acronym for European Committee for Standardization; CENELEC is acronym for European Committee for Electrotechnical Standardization; internal standards-making bodies.

Certification system. Procedures and rules for conducting conformity assessment activities.

Conformance assessment. Also called conformity assessment; testing or evaluating service, process, or product for conformance to requirements.

Conformance assessment modules. Methods for determining the quality of products, services, and processes; quality systems auditing to ISO 9001/9002/9003 is part of the conformity assessment modules.

Conformity. Compliance, fulfillment, or satisfaction of specified process, service, or product requirements.

Corrective action. Actions to eliminate the symptom and the root cause of a nonconformance.

Deficiency. Also called nonconformance; not fulfilling or satisfying an ISO standard requirement.

EC. Acronym for European Community; consists of: Belgium, Denmark, France, Germany, Greece, Ireland, Italy, Luxembourg, Netherlands, Portugal, Spain, and United Kingdom.

EFTA. Acronym for European Free Trade Association; consists of: Austria, Finland, Iceland, Norway, Sweden, and Switzerland.

EN 45000 standards. European Norm certification standards that accreditors, registrars, and laboratories must comply with.

EOTC. Acronym for European Organization for Testing and Certification; promotes mutual recognition for testing and certification.

Global certification. Acceptance of testing and certification results among countries so there is a single, transparent global trade environment.

Harmonization. Term used for standardization in order to create national, regional, and international product compatibility and transparency.

IEC. Acronym for International Electrotechnical Committee; IEC is electrical equivalent of ISO.

Inspection. Method for evaluating conformity (to requirements) by testing, measuring, or observing.

ISO. Acronym for International Organization of Standardization; consists of ninety-one national signatories; ANSI is U.S. representative.

ISO 9000. Formal standard title and application scope is "Quality Management and Quality Assurance Standards: Guidelines for Selection and Use."

ISO 9001. Formal standard title and application scope is "Quality Systems: Model for Quality Assurance in Design/Development, Production, Installation, and Servicing."

ISO 9002. Formal standard title and application scope is "Quality Systems: Model for Quality Assurance in Products and Installation."

ISO 9003. Formal standard title and application scope is "Quality Systems: Model for Quality Assurance in Final Inspection and Test."

ISO 9004. Formal standard title and application scope is "Quality Management and Quality System Elements—Guidelines."

ISO registrars. Bodies recognized, approved, or certified to conduct ISO quality system audits and to maintain lists of approved suppliers.

Laboratory accreditation. Formal recognition and approval of a testing laboratory to conduct specific tests.

Malcolm Baldrige National Quality Award (MBNQA). U.S. national quality award; administered by NIST and ASQC.

Mutual recognition. Agreement between parties to accept testing or other conformity assessment results; recognition set up at international, regional, national, or industry levels.

NIST. Acronym for National Institute for Standards and Technology (USA); formerly National Bureau of Standards (NBS).

NVLAP. Acronym for National Voluntary Laboratory Accreditation Program; NIST-managed industry voluntary program for accrediting testing laboratories.

Process. Set of activities involving inputs, activities, and outputs.

Quality. Multiple definitions include (1) satisfied customer; (2) ability to comply with requirements; and (3) stable processes, etc.

Quality audit. Same as quality systems audit; conformance assessment mechanism where third party, usually a registrar, conducts an assessment to determine compliance with ISO 9000 standards.

Quality audit stages. Three stages of quality audit are (1) Planning; (2) Implementation; and (3) Reporting/Closure.

Quality plan. Quality document describing activities, resources, and sequence of operations to attain, maintain, and improve product or project quality.

Quality system. Required processes, procedures, structure, accountabilities, and resources to implement Total Quality Management.

Quality system documentation. Documents describing organizational quality efforts; may include quality manual, procedures, work instructions, engineering points, quality standards, etc.

RAB. Acronym for Registrar Accreditation Board, an affiliate of ASQC; function is to recognize registrars and quality systems auditors.

Recertification. Registrar requirement that registered companies submit to a full reaudit periodically, usually every three years.

Registration. Also called certification; procedure by which a recognized body verifies that applicable process, service, or product characteristics conform to ISO 9000 requirements; body maintains lists and ensures capability of its auditors.

Registration stages. Three stages of certification or registration, consisting of (1) preregistration; (2) registration; and (3) post registration.

SPC. Acronym for Statistical Process Control; statistical method for monitoring, correcting, and improving processes.

Strategic supplier partnering. View that suppliers are important sources of ideas, resources, designs, and other capabilities for improving one's competitiveness.

Supplier declaration. Supplier provides written assurance that process, service, or product conforms to requirements; sometimes called self-certification.

Surveillance. Periodic, usually every six months, evaluation or assessment of ISO registered quality systems to determine quality requirements are satisfied.

Third party. Recognized, independent, and authoritative group or person conducting tests, audits, or other functions sanctioned by a "first" party and a "second" party.

Total Quality Management. System to use resources economically, effectively, and efficiently so all stakeholders are satisfied; implies total participation, continuous improvement, and innovation.

Type evaluation. Method for evaluating conformity (to requirements) by evaluating one or more representative samples or specimens from a batch, shipment, or production run. Also called type approval.

RESOURCES

Sources for Standards in the U.S.

American National Standards Institute
11 West 42nd St.
13th Floor
New York, NY 10036
(212) 642-4900

American Society for Quality Control
611 East Wisconsin Ave.
Milwaukee, WI 53201
(414) 272-8575

Compliance Engineering
629 Massachusetts Ave.
Boxborough, MA 01719
(508) 264-4208

Global Engineering
1990 M Street, NW
Suite 400
Washington, DC 20036
(800) 854-7179

National Center for Standards and
    Certification Information
U.S. Department of Commerce
Administration Building, Room A629
Gaithersburg, MD 20899
(301) 975-4040

Registrar Accreditation Board
611 East Wisconsin Ave.
Milwaukee, WI 53201
(414) 272-8575

Sources for Standards in the EC

European Committee for Standardization
    (CEN)
European Committee for
    Electrotechnical Standardization
    (CENELEC)
European Organization for Testing and
    Certification (EOTC)
Secretary General's Office
36 rue de Stassart
1050 Brussels, Belgium
(32) (2) 519-6811

European Telecommunications Standards
    Institute (ETSI)
P.O. Box 152
F-06561 Valbonne, France
(33) (92) 94 42 00

International Electrotechnical
    Commission (IEC)
Rue de Varembe 3
P.O. Box 131
CH-1211 Geneva 20, Switzerland
(41) (22) 734 0150

International Organization for
    Standardization
Rue de Varembe 1
CH-1211 Geneva 20, Switzerland
(41) (22) 749-0111

U.S. Registrars (partial list)

ABS Quality Evaluations, Inc.
263 North Belt East
Houston, TX 77060
(713) 873-9400

American Association for Laboratory
    Accreditation
656 Quince Orchard Rd., #304
Gaithersburg, MD 20878
(301) 670-1377

American European Services, Inc.
1054 31st St., NW, Suite 120
Washington, DC 20007
(202) 337-3214

American Gas Association Laboratories
    (AGA Quality)
8501 E. Pleasant Valley Rd.
Cleveland, OH 44131
(216) 524-4990

AT&T Quality Registrar
1259 S. Cedarcrest Blvd.
Allentown, PA 18103
(215) 770-3285

BQS, Inc.
110 Summit Ave.
P.O. Box 460
Montvale, NJ 07645
(800) 624-5892

Bureau Veritas Quality International
509 North Main St.
Jamestown, NY 14701
(800) 937-9311

DNV Industrial Service, Inc.
16340 Park 10 Place, Suite 100
Houston, TX 77084
(713) 579-9003

Intertek
9900 Main St., Suite 500
Fairfax, VA 22031
(703) 476-9000

Perry Johnson Registrars, Inc.
3000 Town Center, Suite 2960
Southfield, MI 48075
(800) 800-0450

KEMA USA
4379 County Line Rd.
Chalfont, PA 18914
(215) 822-4281

Lloyd's Register Quality Assurance, Ltd.
33-41 Newark St.
Hoboken, NJ 07030
(201) 963-1111

MET Electrical Testing Co.
916 W. Patapsco Ave.
Baltimore, MD 21230
(301) 354-2200

National Quality Assurance
1146 Massachusetts Ave.
Boxborough, MA 01719
(508) 635-9256

National Sanitation Foundation
3475 Plymouth Rd.
P.O. Box 130140
Ann Arbor, MI 48106
(313) 769-8010

National Standards Authority of Ireland
5 Medallion Center
Greenley St.
Merrimack, NH 03054
(603) 424-7070

Quality Systems Registrars, Inc.
1555 Naperville/Wheaton Rd.
Naperville, IL 60563
(708) 778-0120

SGS Yarsley Quality Assured Firms
1415 Park Ave.
Hoboken, NJ 07030
(201) 792-2400

Scott Technical Services
34 Channing St.
Suite 400
Newton, MA 02158
(617) 527-7032

Southwest Research Institute
6220 Culebra Rd.
San Antonio, TX 78228
(512) 522-3145

TUV Rheinland of North America, Inc.
12 Commerce Rd.
Newtown, CT 06470
(203) 426-0888

Underwriters Laboratories, Inc.
333 Pfingsten Rd.
Northbrook, IL 60062
(708) 272-8800

Vincotte USA, Inc.
10497 Town & Country Way, Suite 900
Houston, TX 77024
(713) 465-2850

Canadian Registrars (partial list)

Canadian Gas Association
55 Scarsdale Rd.
Don Mills, Ontario M3B 2R3
(416) 447-6465

Canadian General Standards Board
9C1 Phase 3
Place du Portage
11 Laurier St.
Hull, Quebec
(819) 956-0439

Groupement Québecois de Certification
    de la Qualité
220-70 rue Dalhousie
Quebec, Quebec G1K 4B2
Canada
(418) 643-5813

Quality Management Institute
1420 Mississauga Executive Center
2 Robert Speck Parkway
Mississauga, Ontario L4Z 1S1
(416) 272-3920

INDEX